STONE ALTARS

Peter Weltner

Photographs by Nathan Wirth

STONE ALTARS

Editor: Clarinda Harriss
Graphic design: Ace Kieffer

BrickHouse Books, Inc. 2015
306 Suffolk Road
Baltimore, MD 21218

ISBN: 978-1-938144-36-3

Distributor: Itasca Books, Inc.

Printed in the United States of America

For Gerald Coble and Robert Nunnelley

Photographs by Nathan Wirth

buddha and clouds, 2012 (Front Cover)

Light, 2015 (Frontispiece)

buddha & waves, 2015 (p. 10)

The Poet's Tree, 2012 (p. 28)

Deux, 2014 (p. 50)

Into the Fog, 2011 (p. 72)

light & water, 2015 (p. 114)

Minstrels, 2009 (Back Cover)

Table of Contents

III

IV

V

I

A Promise

A curved, black, spindle back chair. A once plush red
cushion faded to rose-soft orange or pink. A pale
olive green sweater drapes over it. The floor boards–shed,
barn dark–are centuries old. Tan, like a rusted nail,
two shoes, work boots, laces untied, rest. Ceramic
cups, a bowl for cats. A part of a chair, carved
arms, the paint worn smooth, no wood exposed. A hutch, thick
slats, built solid. One door's swung open. It's piled
with stacks of white or gray porcelain bowls and plates.
On its side, the weathered wood of an antique ironing board
hangs from a nail. The ghost of a snow shovel waits
out the glass door propped on a wall. Old things adored,
the snow shining bright as a flashbulb. So ancient deeds burn
through time. I promise. He's just stepped out. He'll soon return.

Prospero to Faustus

We two: fortunate, book lovers, magicians. You,
the rebel. I, rebelled against. All arts
are dark. Remember those we harmed, the hearts
we ruined by our solitude? I thought to rescue
a few I shipwrecked off my island. You plotted
with Mephisto to show how men are dupes and fools.
The trick's the same. We lived by our own rules.
Yet how weak's the power an artist's allotted.
You died terrified. Now I'm home, afraid, with no
spells or spirits left me. Children misrule the state.
I'm confused. I think of you, with nowhere to go.
Were we truly fortunate, Faustus, who lived too late,
past magic? After the first death there is no other,
a poet wrote. Forgive me and be forgiven, brother.

An Old Man Sleeps in Yadkin County

Furry, boneless, a squirrel's flattened pelt
is drying on the white line of a country road.
Its shoulder's collapsing into kudzu. His boy's belt
holds up the slacks his mother's re-sewed.

The leaves are browning. Trees shade what they can.
The narrow path, scrub grass, dried clay,
starts nowhere, follows no clear plan,
meanders through weeds. He's lost the day,

what year it is, in the woods' spare light.
Grey mosses, leafy lichen cling to bark
and boulders. Leaves spiral down like his kite
when its string was sliced by wires in the dark,

like winged seeds in spring in back
of his house or by the creek, like paper
airplanes drifting to ground, a track
of jets dispersing, snow flakes in winter,

falling freely. A creek zigzags down slick
red clay, its steep, sheer bank a wall
of brush and rhododendron. The trick
is to hold onto vines and not slip or fall.

Gnats swarm over the trickling water
where a skate darts like a trapped fly.
He crawls in the cave–rank as wet fur,
dank, spider-webbed, five feet high–

and lights a match. There's a rust red
wound in its side no bigger than
a bullet hole, the body of a dead
thing lying on the floor. It looks human.

This is where his terrors have always
led him, to this youthful crime, a cavern,
a den, where his sin, his guilt betrays
itself as death does, how it fits a pattern

he can't abide where it's never day.
Outside's more woods, a dirt road along
a fallow field curving away
from a rust-stained farm house, from the wrong

he's done it, its broken shutters, its shades drawn,
frayed, its paint curled like wood shavings.
A woman answers his knock. "My son,
my son," she says, and kisses him. Then sings.

Or keens. With a long wood spoon, she points
to a weathered plank bridge. "There, there's
where you once played and swam." Her joints
crack as she steps back. He stares

at a faded road sign: *The young for the old*.
When the boy reaches the creek, he kneels
on a rock. The water as ever is cold,
bitter, thigh-high from the late rain swells.

He is praying it were his bedtime. Thirsty,
he scrambles down the bank, cups his hands.
Blinded by sunlight, he kneels on one knee.
The water tastes salty. LIke ocean sands.

Like brine. Like blood. It seeps downstream
from where a man is shoveling clay. To bury
what? How does he end a dream,
a story of the boy he was? He must hurry,

must run away, must flee the past,
its haunting memories, escape its pain,
its indelible wrong. How long must it last,
this vision he's seen of what's been slain?

A shovel glints where the man is digging.
What lured the boy to the cave in the woods?
Who died there? Why go back? Can a thing
he couldn't have done be so? Blood's

on his hands, stains his soul, his brain,
paints his future the same scab-like red.
He's filled with dread–the panic, the pain
the dead must feel the moment they're dead.

No matter how unclear, the boy believes
what he's been shown, fears what he fears,
on his knees begs God, utters pleas
to him, implores him with prayers and tears

as he returns to the woods, the cave
past the rusted house, the bridge, the stream,
the grieving mother, father, the grave
he keeps digging. There's nothing to redeem

the man, sleeping uneasily the restless
sleep of one who can't quit being
asleep, yet needing to confess
to what he didn't do, this thing

of sin, guilty, guiltless, an old man,
a young boy, the past he struggles to
awake from, deny, as no sleeper can,
the cave where is lying what mustn't be true.

Darl Bundren, Home from France

The war was like home, Mississippi,
unraveling, spilling, a stuck hog's guts
slopping a tub. Ben's blasted knee,
Dalton tangled on the wire, Clay's nuts

blown off, floating in a moon-lit pool,
Leith burning up. It was a Mississippi
rain they died in, a runny stool
of mud the color of sassafras tea,

bi-planes hungry as buzzards. My mother
never loved me. My dad's like God,
feckless, lazy, toothless, more a bother
to his kids than a comfort. I guess I'm odd.

No use with tools. My fishing rod
catches nothing. I'm good as dead,
bayoneted. Where's the watch, the gold fob
I bought in Paris? Flies buzz in my head.

Maybe it's a whizbang . Maybe it's time.
Back home, I've got three brothers, a sister.
But I was born in France, in the slime,
the muck, the roiling muddy water

flooding trenches with blood. I like a nice inn,
an estaminet, a glass of red wine,
a bed of my own where I can sin
if I I want to miles away from the line

and listen to the rain on a strange roof
and think of home and how it's the same
here as there, war the only truth,
the way the world's been made. My name

is Darl. Darl is my brother, too. You are
Darl also, like Dalton, caught, pricked
by the barbs, Clay, balls flung far,
high up, dropping beside me, Leith tricked

into running too soon by the sun. Buddies.
Someone's friend, if not mine. Alone, I stare
through walls trying to see how He sees
the world, even Mississippi where

no one's ever at home and the train
I ride in goes backwards to France
and in the hot July sun the rain
pours up from the earth. Luck, chance,

like jokes, make me laugh. Insanity?
My brother Cash tells me I'm out
of balance. But if flood, fire can't bury
the dead, why not cry or shout

or laugh? At you. At God. At the war
in my head that never stops, won't quit,
that sticks and burns like roofing tar
on Cash's skin. Like cement on bone. I sit

in my room in Jackson, sharp as a knife
I'm told, and hear the lies they say. *Be
peaceful, brother. The war, that life,
France is over. You're home. It's Mississippi.*

Winter Solstice

1.
All is white. A woman on a gurney. His own gown
(open in back), the curtains, walls, a clock face
and hands, the buzzing light above him. White. Down
a hall, nurses murmur. A muffled laugh. In a trace
of a sigh, he hears a northern breeze in late
winter. Noon is bleaching the sky. His mind's
a blank, blurred as the spinning colors of a wheel,
the no colors of words. What's his name, his date
of birth? There's no him left to speak of. As he winds
through corridors, the floors he walks on tip like the keel
of a ship. Back in bed, he flips on his side, bites
on a bit with a hole for a tube. White waves. His sight's
set northward. White tides roll in. He's trying to stay
in the Arctic. Snow is blissful. The white nights of Norway.

2.
The sun is hiding in a field of mice and corn stubble.
A chill wind. The old man wheezes in his bed.
He struggles up from his swaybacked mattress. Trouble
is coming. It's Satan down the road, his eyes red,
glowing above the horizon, below the pine stand.
Cold seeps through his windows, cripples the hand
the Lord has blessed. He's healed the infirm, ill,
and broken, not by his skill, but by God's. It's a miracle
he's stayed saved and sin-free. Oh, preacher man, who knows
righteous anger, the gospels by heart, the folly
of these times, the Word, who, in the dark, shows
the way: your grandson, scion of your blood–see
what you've done–his drawers torn down to his knees,
his cheeks lipstick smeared, lies unrisen like the sun in trees.

December, 1962

After Thanksgiving in '62 the trees, the streams,
fields, quads, hills, turned to white. In dreams,

we'd been made a promise that couldn't be kept: the snow
would melt early that year if, in the cemetery below

the chapel, the men, boys, a few women from the College,
slept undisturbed, no one joining them by the edge

of the campus. The roads ash-gray, covered with cinders,
the walk ways, coal black, it was the worst of winters,

the drifts piling head high as early as mid-December.
The crash happened before the break, Kit, Cam, Winger

(though Tom survived it), a pile-up in a blizzard
on the New York Thruway. A slash, a sudden fissure,

a rupture between worlds. The snow was rafter-high
around the Sig House after Kit's funeral. Irony,

our way of life, became useless. His mother, father
in the middle of a circle of his real and frat brothers,

their girls, all quiet. No one knew what to do or say.
Fresh snow shone like May into the room, the day

outside brilliant, icy white, a blue-cast
to it, a clear, close light like spring's. It didn't last.

The next night, a blast felled the tallest tree
in Root Glen. From a window in South Dorm, I could see

it fall. I watched how it died. The snow below it
exploded, then drifted back down. The big elm, split

apart by the wind's force, was buried under
a pall of white and disappeared. A trick of winter

is to make you feel safe inside, a fire
burning in the hearth in your room. Cam Myers,

Kit Miner, dead at twenty. The snow wouldn't quit
the night they were killed. The truck driver who hit

their car couldn't see it. It was invisible, like nothing,
a white out. Bright as sun on ice, his headlights, shining

on a snow pile, blinded him. Or blame absence,
winter's early dark, its cold, its silence.

Late October, 1959

1.

He yearns in his memory of it for more, craves
more details, more dialogue, more friends in it,
seeks more particulars, the dailiness that saves
the past from vanishing into night after the half-lit
shadows at dusk, that welcomes dawn, morning,
the school day just beginning, birds aloft in the light,
cars on the road, people on buses, crowding
the sidewalks hurrying to work, the strange sight
of kids half-woken up, their nightly slumbers over
until darkness and sleep descend again. Even
the uncertainty of what's ahead's no matter. It's the power
of lives recalled he's longing for, the heaven
of the usual, the common, the sun that sings
in October of young bodies and places and things.

2.

He's standing today where he stood twenty years
before and often five decades ago. It's fall.
Little's changed. Suddenly in front of him appears
himself, seventeen. The school, classrooms, hall
he lingers in, staring out a window, are the same,
the trees' leaves just turning oak orange or maple
red, his long life to come calling out his name
as a friend might, something so plain, simple
about friendship then, so kind when he thinks
of it now, despite his old loneliness. The lockers,
their gun metal gray unchanged, the faucets, sinks
in the chemistry room are as rusty. Like clockers,
a few teachers spy on the walkways, still time how long
their students dawdle, envy what they're doing wrong.

3.

The parking lot is crowded with cars. Yellow
school buses line up below the football field.
He's standing on a bleacher. How can he know

the meaning of what fails to alter or yield
to time? The stadium is exactly the same,
too, like the auditorium with its WPA murals
and plywood-like uncushioned seats. The past is shame-
less the way it clings dustily to ceilings, walls
and floors. He hears sounds like yearbook photos
or Miss Madlin's voice teaching him Latin syntax,
immutable, permanent–the pictures she shows
to her class, the maps of Rome, eternal facts
he learns by translating Caesar, Ovid, Cicero,
learning of ancient ways he's told he'll outgrow.

4.

The air's spare, tawny, an October afternoon
smell to it like the delights of Halloween,
though he and his friends, all seniors, are too old too soon
for trick or treating. It's the same light he'd seen
in woods as a child when the trees were chang-
ing and the sun took on its own autumn colors
even at noon, a Rembrandt light, the strange
sheen of a painting painted in old age that favors
the gleam in eyes to the shine of young bodies.
He stands at the end of the Science building, listening
to Jabbo preach about physics. What he sees
instead of the experiment his teacher's performing
is the light outside, not at eight or twelve or three
fifteen, but a day being what it will always be.

5.

From a page of Tennyson, a dreary, nocturnal,
romantic meditation on friendship and oblivion,
he looks anxiously up at Miss Joyner. She does call
on him next. He wonders what to say, if he'd done
enough already that class, an accomplishment
of sorts, just understanding the poem–the dread
that is existence, the loss, whatever is meant
by before and after, presentiments said
to belong to God or his holy ones. Not yet,

for him, the deep unknowing, the past surging
into the poet's thoughts by the death of his friend. Forget
it, Lord T., he'd callously say. It's everything
he's not, not yet, sitting in a classroom, mur-
muring beneath his breath lines he'll need years later.

6.
As Rick's rooms become fewer, smaller, the more ill
he is, his mind weakens. His days are nightmares
that haunt him awake with cold, strident, shrill
voices that force him to raise his, the dread that dares
him to become what he was never before, shrew-
shrill, who when his stricken boyfriend comes
in his wheelchair to visit him will always do
the impossible—stick out his tongue. His home's
long lost. He's shrunken to no size. He shits
in his diapers, wipes it on his thighs and knees.
This is what the boy could never imagine he'd see,
friends dying young like the most ruined old be-
come, their lives mere mutterings, a mad language
of ravings, of youth betrayed, its confusions and rage.

7.
At the border between now and then, the word
not otherwise spoken, the music not otherwise
sounded, a Schubert sonata perhaps, the third
from the last, the one in C minor: no lies,
no illusions possible in such music, profundities
revealed not given to words, reserved for night,
dreams, memories, whatever one needs to seize
the past, to bring it back, to make it right,
true if you like, unburdened by the impurities
of human speech, the music of another sense,
better for saying what we mean and cannot
say, how it is his youth that lingers in the lim-
inal half-light and shadows of a dying man's
work, mourning a time he too late understands.

8.

This is a poem for Lindley, Corb, many others,
schoolmates he'd failed too often, Lester, Bob,
Sherry, Walton, Dan, Cricket, like lovers
of his later years, Anne, Shannon, Rob-
ert, Julie, Tony, friends seen by a certain
strain of light, late October's, the orange sun
dying into red over the trees, stain-
ing their faces with a burning glow, each one
still young, brighter in the twilight than they are by
day because he who writes, old now, holds onto dreams
and images that cling to his mind like a white lie
he tells to himself, because otherwise the past seems
to escape him, as love does, unless he's true to desire,
to memories like fall leaves at sunset, doubly on fire.

For M in Ireland

Not yet too old for it, he falls in love with another
man. His wife of many fulfilling years is ill,
unable to care for herself anymore. Water
is what the soul is made of. He watches it spill
like rain from a gutter. His beloved's off to Galway.
Such passion as he's never known. The rivers fill,
overflow their banks. It's dark as night this day
in Ireland. He stands distraught on a Dublin hill,
contemplates time like a storm at sea. He must
be good. Rain and more rain's the weather of his life.
Let it pour. Let it thrill him like lightning, a tempest,
a shipwreck. The best he can wish for now is strife,
the pain inside him. Or is it a kindness, like grace,
that makes him shudder? A man's kiss, a sick wife's embrace.

My Mother in Her Dotage and the Kindness of the Lord

She hefts her dress up, tugs on her right stocking,
exposing a thigh and her diapers. The Beauty Queen
natters on about her victory in the 'thirties, shocking
no one anymore. Sid Cone insists he's just seen

the ghost of his cousin Claribel, but he seems
to have mistaken her for Gertrude Stein.
The widow in black tells each detail of her dreams
as if she'd spent the whole night shopping. A fine,

strapping old man is prompted to sing a hymn.
He swings his arms as if he means us all
to join in. Some do, from table to table, at the whim
of the moment, until everyone, the whole dining hall,

is singing "Abide with Me" and my mother is crying
not at the song but at her loss of dignity,
her hair unbrushed for days, her hearing aids buzzing,
urine dribbling down despite her diapers. "To be

old," she whispers to me, "is horrible." And I think
of her and my father, making loving, making me.
It was in their pleasure my life began. Sink,
I'd say to her, sink back, drown now in that ecstasy.

A Last Trip Back from the Veterinary Hospital

1.
She scratches an ear. Her snout's whiskery grizzled.
She'd been abused before we adopted her, abandoned,
teats distended, had just had pups, seemed muzzled
at first. It took awhile before she'd bark. We were stunned
by how deep her voice was, how often joyful, a signal
she expected her bowl to be filled, with lots of treats
after. We turn away from the Pacific, walk down
the dunes, avoid the ice plants. Each step repeats
in my dream her careful way, slow pace: brown
thoughts at night like daytime's gold. Nora, I say, pal,
and tug the leash impatiently to hurry her on. But no.
Even with breakfast just a few blocks away, there's much
to discover. Haste isn't her style. She prefers the world slow.
We three are watching a show on TV. I touch
her gently, softly rub her belly. There's much I don't know
about what's not like me. Like her. I say, Good gal,

good Nora. With eyes more astute than humans',
she sees us. Sleeps in our bed, rests on our couch,
our sofa. Goes with us wherever we go, Land's
End, Sea Ranch, Point Reyes. Woefully out of touch
with animal feelings, I often mistake her mean-
ings. She likes to play, but exhibits a Rott's dignity,
some Lab in her to sweeten the mix. She had no clean
start with us, never forgets the earlier blows, might see
in dark places the cellar in which she'd been imprisoned.
Kindness may say as much as love, but fear
has left its wounds on her. Quietly scolded,
she'll jump on a bed and cower. Cowers. She's not here
when I wake up. Spinal myelopathy. The decline
she endures, as I never could, happy, fine
much of the time, though at the end unable to walk,
unable to move, in pain, uncomplaining. Don't talk,
she seems to say, resigned on the gurney as Atticus
and I try futilely to bid goodbye. We kiss her,

pet her, find no words. She carefully studies us,
her eyes clouded by cataracts, like soapy water,
blinks a few times, and falls asleep. It takes only
seconds. Why do I see her die again this morning,
when, look, she's lying at the foot of my bed? We
are not done, Nora, Atticus, and I. It's raining.
She and I hide under a tall sycamore in the park
to keep from getting wetter. A rat scurries by.
She jerks on her leash. There's something better
to do, a smelly furry gray thing to chase, a lark
of sorts. For once, she leads the way. She can't die
quite. Nor can I. Mysteriously we're one. The wetter
the day the more she likes it. More puddles to try,
to lap up, that she prefers to her bowl's, who knows why.

2.
Nora-Belle is sniffing the melting pelt of a feral cat
by Chain of Lakes Drive in Golden Gate Park,
tail-wagging switches to the gopher holes that
ring a stop sign like mini crop circles. It's dark
in my room. Wet grass dirties her paws. I clean
them off with a paper towel and try to guide
her onto the walk, free from tempting smells. Sprinklers
fan the rhododendron and fern trees. I coax her beside
me, but she chooses to dawdle behind. The odor is hers
I smell on my bed, in my sleep. On a dune, a torn
child's t-shirt, a dirty sock attract her exploring
while I watch the sea. Behind me, at first light, the forlorn
cry of gulls. Nora looks up at me, sits. Am I boring
her? Dawn is tinting the white water rose pink.
A cliché, I guess. I'm crying. What must she think?
Does a dog, dreaming, weep? Or only a human being?

3.
After his dog had died, Dan Weiss
said to Steve Arkin, "I loved having
Dylan with me. He seemed to forgive
me for being who I am."

Our dog died yesterday, dies twice
in my dreams where it seems death is nothing,
or the nothing that would live
beyond its span. Old Abraham,

founder, father, paid a high price
for all he would have, accepting
God's command of filicide, no reprieve
given him, were it not for the ram.

4.
The soot-blackened smoke slowly fades to the gray
of wet cement as it dissipates above
The Great Highway, drifting like mist toward the Bay.
The air is smoggy, a muggy evening, no sign of
March in such unseasonable weather. Maybe
the fire was deliberately set or perhaps someone
carelessly dropped a cigarette or joint. The dunes' sea
oats, grass, ice plants, two blocks wide, are done
for, fried to a crisp, the sand black as sun-
baked seaweed from the embers. Memory
is often like that. Something you love is burned
to ash. You hold her in your lap enclosed in a pine
box, her name inscribed in black on a shiny, fine
brass plaque. All you know is black. Black is all you've learned.

Four Showers

1.

Water-worn rocks, sandstone smooth, speckled,
onto which a stream pours, a pounding cascade
falling on the boy's back and shoulders, his dirt-freckled,
ruddy face scrubbed to a shine in the half-shade
of rhododendron, a dark thicket of ivy, brush,
and honeysuckle. There's no path to the roaring shower,
no trail. The boy's drawn there by luck, by the lush
summer overgrowth and the fall's power.
As in the stall back home, he waits until, feeling
the water change him, he's draining through
the trap or into the swirl below, the pool healing
him of his wounds and terrors, making him new,
a boy turned into cascading water, the light of it
glittering in his eyes, its flow, its amazement.

2.

In muted sunshine, in ancient woods back
of his home, during a thunderstorm in August,
lightning burning through leaves, no trace left, no track
of his way in, he smells wet stones, attic must,
old damp clothes in the air. Beneath a hole
in the canopy, like a run away, naked
as an animal on the needle strewn ground, mole-
blind to all but the bolts of lightning shed
from the sky, dead branches from trees crashing
to earth, trying to hide, he finds a pool
in which he rolls like a dog in mud, thrashing
about having found a way to get cool
on a simmering day, in a scary storm, to be
drenched bone-wet, dirty, yet amazingly free.

3.

In a Ventura motel, during the Ojai festival,
after a night of Ives and Stravinsky in the shell,
he and Bob shower together in a small

stall they barely fit in, scrubbing fast, but well,
each others' backs and chests, lingering on
parts farther below, the hot water steaming,
prickling their skin, red from the heat, from the run
of blood through their bodies, the rush of seed streaming
through flesh and spilling onto the showers'
floor where it mingles with the soapy water
and twirls round the drain like petals from flowers
in a run-off after a storm, their laughter
spinning, too, as they stare down in amazement
at how much jizz into the swirling pool they've spent.

4.
Harsh storms are coming. Mother of god, mistress
of heaven, see clouds blacken. Soon he will shiver
in the cold. You care for sailors in distress.
Ocean-bearer, whose tears are stream and river,
urn-carrier who pours down the rain the living need
onto the ground, into mouths, wash his sweat
and grime away, chill his fevers. You feed
the greedy for nourishment. The boy's grown old. Let
him still drink from your breast. Near and far,
you shower blessings on what grieves, you to whom
nature flees in tribulation, in flight from history,
its rubble and ash, its broken stones, the sealed tomb.
All truth is sexual. Let it rain amazement on sea
and land. Free us. Release the waters that we are.

Le Quattro Stagioni

1. Spring

An April light you can hear, like mist at dawn
on a canal. The sun shines softly on basilica
gold, its ivory tawny as an antique chess pawn.
An orphan girl's lips ripen as she yawns. Fa
sol la. It shines from a new wig or silk breeches.
Stage candles illuminate the action's scene,
its plot of mistaken identities. A daughter beseeches
her father to forgive her captured lover, so keen
on revenge. Or is he his son? Forget, forgive.
Three women are rivals for the same man. Orlando
is mad again. Caio rages. Who will live,
who die? The libretto's by Metastasio,
as operatic as Venice, as my last night's dream.
Suppose life were sung. How much more real it might seem.

2. Summer

Fantasies. I'm two men, both of them, on their way
to a family picnic in Texas. The lanky blond one's
parents don't know he's gay. I tell me what to say.
I can make all things right. I am the stones
Saint Anne de Beaupré's pilgrims reach out to touch.
Holiness is mine to give and convey. Or I may be
a lover groping in the dark, trying to clutch
closer a man so ghostly, so elusive I'll never see
him by lamp or daylight. I'll hold him all the tighter
whenever he claims he's unreal. I am a red priest
capable of miraculous healing, a teacher, a fighter
for the peaceful. I am a music that's as wild or at least
as free as jazz or baroque is, improvisationally
formal. I'm a rain-filled drought-killing sky in late July.

3. Fall

In the autumn of his life, no longer writing,
taking no more pictures, Wright Morris listened on
an old record player–his mind, his hearing
slowly failing–to Mahler and Vivaldi. Now he's gone,
I wish I'd asked him why he chose those two
whom I find myself listening to more and more
for solace, I suppose, or consolation. Life's not through
with me yet, but I've grown bored and a bore.
Cum dederit dilectis suis somnum.
For so he gives his beloved sleep. Vivaldi,
Mahler, dreamers of a would-be world. Fingers numb
from picking eggs, cutting wire, the smell of dung
tainting his clothes, work to make a child cry,
in wind, heat, dust, Will's boy hears plains' song.

4. Winter

Just one concerto repeated six hundred times
or six hundred concerti? What if repetition
is invention, our days and years how life rhymes?
We live out our seasons in endless imitation
of what has come before us and what will follow,
by heart beat and breath and the pulse of intercourse.
The past is the future. Time's a transcription. So fallow
fields in winter yield their mystical lambs and grain.
So desire flows below an iced-in river to its source,
a spring-time fountain, pastoral, without the stain
of old age when your body is and isn't the same.
Like a chaconne or passacaglia, you sound your changes
on a ground bass theme. Listen to Vivaldi's B flat
major concerto. What is a self, what's in a name,
if you become what you hear? What if age arranges
you to be the tune that is most you. What if life is that.

Jim Bergeron, Seen through Sea Oats

Naked, skinnier, Jim lies in wheat-high grass
on a balmy May morning, basking in the sun.
If I could, I'd ask him to stay, not let him pass
us by, departing from all he's meant or done.

As if delayed, a ship lingers, waiting on the horizon.
When I look up again, it's disappeared, who knows
where. I miss him awfully. After the first lesion
showed on his face, he vanished. Wherever life goes,

it's always mutable, like dunes, shape-shifting,
changing with the wind every day. The Great Highway
is closed because of sand on the road drifting
across. He wanted to write. He had much to say

about his days in New Orleans, in San Francisco later,
the abuse he knew, his wild lovers, his disease.
Naked, skinny, Jim lies in wheat-high grass, a blur,
like a child half-hiding, playing in a pile of leaves.

Michael's Gift

A plaster cow and donkey, five sheep, one chipped,
two shepherds chopped from pine, their crooks
twisted oak limbs, the magi garbed in silk ripped
from old scarves. Joseph's badly faded. Mary looks
downcast with re-painted doll-like eyes. The baby
Jesus is wrapped in cotton swaddles. The palms
are plastic. So's the manger in the cave. Michael can see
it's backlit like a stage, not by the star. What qualms
he feels as he ponders the shoddy nativity scene
in the church yard are not calmed when his mother
whispers in his ear, "It's Christmas, son. Hell's
shut down for folks like us, heaven-bound." Mean-
ing what? Could it be really true there's another
world less sad than this? Be good, he's told, or else.

He's bullied at school, called a gay boy, a faggot by
the tougher guys. He never wants or means to stare.
They beat him with willow switches, make him cry,
leave him hurt and dirty in an arroyo. He doesn't care
his teachers think him lazy during classes.
He's tall, strong, but hates to fight and knows more
than other kids, stumbles sometimes, wears glasses,
boasts he doesn't believe in God anymore, would implore
Him to make them quit it if he did. Is it selfish
of him to pray for himself when he doesn't even try
to stop abusing himself? Maybe he'll die. It's absurd
the world's unkind. "Make a wish, make a wish,"
his mother says. "It's your birthday." With a sigh,
he blows out the candles. They must know, have heard

of why he's bullied. It's past time. He runs away,
leaves Corpus Christi to the morons, takes a bus
to Frisco, crashes in a pad, is invited to stay
in a derelict Victorian where gay hippies fuss
over him like a baby. He needs to escape
after a few days. What they do is sin. He'd lose

his soul if he were to succumb. "God's what you make
of yourself," his mother had said. "What you choose."
But he's chosen to defy her the Christmas I meet
him in the Capri, nursing a ginger ale. Great genes,
I think. In my bedroom, naked, only a cross
round his neck, he begs me to let us greet
the new year together since the crowd scenes
in gay bars scare him, fill him with a sense of loss.

We date for three months. It's fine. I don't know why
I feel it can't last. He finds a job in Fields Book-
store, likes to cook, go to movies, try
new trails in west Marin. He's very good look-
ing, though he isn't persuaded when I say
so. But I tell him to leave anyway. I stop calling
him, dropping by his room on a bay-
side alley off the Embarcadero. Everything
I do is hurtful. I'm just one more mean school
yard bully, a trite, blaspheming, uncaring lover
who abuses his love by looking for another
better than him. Better than Mike? From the letter
he writes after he's left, I know I'm a fool.
He's enclosed the cross he wore, still a believer.

May each of us, at the end of our days, be spared
the wrath of our cruelties, the rage of memory's
curse, reminding us of our unkindness, those who cared
for us whom we failed. We, who do only what pleases
us, may we be forgiven for not loving enough,
for achieving only what was convenient,
what desire sought, who believed we could bluff
our way past death and need never repent.
In our last hour, relieve our minds and souls
of our hard words, each unkind, uncaring thing
we've said and done, you, who are music, who sing
in imagination, the angel fable says controls
our final moments, save us as we die, preserve
the love, the gifts we were given and didn't deserve.

West from the Bay

1. Golden Gate Bridge

Foghorns groan. They're moaning from below the ocean,
old bones or Tennyson's kraken. Sirens sound near-
by, though they don't scare him. He's there to lean
precariously over the railing. A life is made clear-

er when it starts to fall. The stories, the art that make
it seem right plummet into the sea, for bad
or good, unmoored by waves. His life feels a fake.
Who is he to pretend he could save her? She's mad.

She believes in her poems and her husband's. Just those.
And in enemies. Thirty nine years ago, they stood
on the Golden Gate Bridge. He might have torn off his clothes
and jumped. The appeal of water is like a falsehood

he's compelled to tell and can't stop telling. She held
his hand as they walked back to safety and his car.
She recited a sad poem she'd written. The waves swelled
over the road. It was the day after the end of the war.

2. Lookout over Baker Beach

A row of bunkers waits years later
for an army that never comes, slumbering
like tombstones, by which a man stands, pondering
the beach below, hollowed like a bomb crater

by an invading sea that puts in harms'
way sky, sunlight, air, the undeep
things it lulls too easily asleep,
the boys it's snatched from their parents' arms.

3. A Strong Spring Wind off the Bay

His books are piled in stacks as high as the backs
on straight chairs. Though time won't let him read them
all, he still buys more, so many that he racks
his brain trying to recall where they are. Remem-

ber what the future glibly promised years ago?
Clichés. Art's long, life's short. The art part isn't
really so. On his deck, he hears the wind blow
through the Golden Gate. A glass bowl's a prism,

refracting twilight. Most books die faster than
whoever writes them. Play tag if you can, little
boy. Why should it matter who's an old man?
Play tag if you can. The wind carries the spittle

he spits into it like seeds on the wing he watches
fly free. There's a music in its gusts he could use.
He scribbles some French with a stick in thick patches
of dust on the redwood. *Je ne suis pas heureuse.*

Lost Mélisande. Debussy's in his head. *Children's
Corner*, the faun, the sea. In an earthquake, all
of his books would fall and bury him. There are sirens
close by for the tsunami. Let them call him in. Let them call.

4. Ocean Beach

The ice plant's in bloom. The ships sit on the horizon.
The waves sound like traffic, the traffic like waves.
He knows all this, this truth, my son,
who sits in his room doing nothing.

5. Lookout on Mount Tamalpais

There's no wind. The day is clear, still, airless.
he bends his ear toward it as he did to hear
his father's last words when he'd little breath left. "Say yes,
my friend, to no more fear. It's a bright new year."

When Stefan went insane, he stepped on land's end's rocks
so anxiously because he knew he'd fall through
the spaces in between into the Absolute. Flocks
of pelicans in their strict formation are flying to

the headlands northwest. The beach is a cemetery,
broken grave markers, the Prince Philip's hull,
sand, shells, buried fin whales, driftwood, sea-
weed, jellyfish baking in the sun. He tries to cull

from nature what he is able to pray to. To take back
his hopes from crows. The moon he woke to
has dropped from the sky, between him and a crack
in the earth. He thinks of dying with quick eyes, true

to Stef, his sights set on the view they hiked to Tam's summit
for, the Pacific from the make-do lookout tower
of the storm-bent oak they climbed–infinite, no limit
to it, as Stef'd promised they'd see, now and in the hour.

6. Fort Point

Youth's a green country west from the bay,
no longer voyageable to, now its islands
have fallen beneath the sea. Some day,
perhaps, they'll rise again. Who understands

this understands all, looking out beyond
the Golden Gate or at the rocks below,
like a man departing, tightening his bond
with the ocean, the love of tides for undertow.

Galen's Glasses

He hikes up river to where it's being drained for rice fields.
Does every stream in the world dream of itself untamed?
He removes his glasses, lays them on a rock, like shields
set aside as a pledge of a truce. A man cannot be blamed

if he looks at the world, sees it, and leaves it unharmed.
For hours, he searches for the waters that are his source,
but back at the rock he finds his glasses are missing. Alarmed,
frustrated, for two days he tries to locate them. The course

of the Maenam is his vision, where his art's origins are hidden.
Must he buy a new pair? For the third time, wearily, he returns
to look for his lost ones. Magnificent, venomous, unbidden,
lying across his path, a large Thai cobra waits. Who learns

to revere from fear is snake-wise. It unfolds its glorious hood,
then, like the river, winds away. He finds his glasses at his feet,
the good surprise, no flood, but waters rising slowly as they should,
reverence, the serpentine wonder, the earth mysterious, complete.

After Sappho, Translated by William Carlos Williams

1.
Mt. Tamalpais,
too green for Greece, and yet
heaven-lit

like a dream of peace
on fire in the sunset
behind it,

the sound of goat carts
in my ears as I watch
children play

in the clouds, their hearts
set on trying to catch
the last day.

2.
Wind, fog-drenched, not rain
but mist's drizzling to cool
the morning

air where, see, again,
boys in a swimming pool,
sleek sweat cling-

ing to skin like oil
on a naked wrestler,
Pindar's Greece

or Sappho's, unspoil-
ed youth. Epic matter
of gold fleece

filched on a hellbent
trip or Odysseus, old
but alive

44

to desire, what he's meant
to find at home as told
in her wiv-

ing him by Penelope,
spared more journeys, illness
at forty,

fifty, later, be-
ing roused by her prowess,
sex's fury.

3.
Weather then, summer
at my lake fifty-five
years ago,

is today's, though hotter
here, clearer, more alive
despite no

thunderstorms mid-aft-
ernoon, no fireflies
by evening.

Old love causes laugh-
ter in the young, the sighs,
tears, pining,

pain, madness best left
to them, their bodies stronger,
beauty-blessed.

But Aphrodite's deft
at her art. All belong to her,
all obsessed,

like me beachside, untrue
to my years, hearing it sung,
forbidden,

what the Sirens knew,
Odysseus heard as he hung—
though didn't

flinch, ropes slicing through
his flesh—at the mast, strung
up by crew,

not yearning for new
love but her he has clung
to, held to

like wind to sails, blue
skies to sun, boys still young
to wise men:

at mere sight of you
my voice falters, my tongue
is broken.

4.
So I, old, worn, no
hero, hear myself pray
to the sea,

horizon, unbro-
ken sky, "May you stay
long by me,

my husband, at sight
of whom words fail me like
memory

of when, at twilight,
thunder, lightning would strike
in July,

my future like a dream
of time, stories of love
I'd tell to

the night, to the steam
rising like the smoke of
fires to you."

5.
Waves unerringly
roar, the Pacific I
walk beside

daily, ancient sea,
now reaching for its high-
est known tide,

old as Sappho's, though
wilder, vaster, more dan-
gerous to

voyage on, not you,
but him, rushing through rain
to someone new.

Deconsecration

No more altar, vestments, stained glass.
The last cross is taken from the church.
Broken plaster lies where the font was.
A priest in a white-washed world, you search

for the black you wore, the dirge you sang
as if it were all the liturgy meant
when in the bell tower the bells rang
and no one came and no one went,

the marriage ended between him and you,
as love sometimes quits between lovers,
God having left the place, who knew
your refusal, all that suffering uncovers,

reveals in the heart, the sanctuary
unattended to, the hymns unsung,
too few in the pews, the daily
strain of unlocking the doors, the tongue

silenced by unbelief, the slow deadening
pace of days. Outside, the homeless
line up for meals, patiently waiting,
the mouths to feed, the sores to bless.

At the Start of Another War

An owl with a vole in its beak
is more than suffering,
is whatever's greater
than an owl's need to eat,
an appetite for pain,
the cruel other thing
hunger also is, the vole
tormented in defeat.

A boy watches in the forest
he's hiding in, a child
straining his eyes
as light yields to dark,
not trying to find his way home
out of wilderness, curious
how the vole's devoured whole,
why the owl leaves no mark,
but perches discontent, insatiable,
in the fattest of the trees,
an oak whose scarily mocking,
pocked face and hairy limbs,
finger-like twigs, toe-like roots,
the boy believes,
are starved for an owl as the owl
for a vole. Or him. The whims

of deep woods and quickening night fall on
the boy like snow.
He shivers
as the vole did dying.
In a clearing, by his feet,
lie slivers
of bone picked clean–
pure, moon white, and keening.

The Day the War Begins Again

1.
A place
like a tower a desperate man climbs, fantasies
of falling, or a bridge to drive across to drown
in, in the flow of traffic, never looking below, down
into the river, afraid of confession, what terrifies
most, the desert winds, the silences of space.

2.
Premonitions
of Paris, London in ruins, cities the mission's
to destroy, the West, the gates back barred,
sunset sneaking through a shade, a bird
light, feathery orange, downy red, heard
behind a house, a child crying in a schoolyard.

3.
As the war begins,
what sins
you don't know yet, a boy on a playground swing
and a girl on a teeter-totter
who keep swaying,
their mother,
father spinning round and round
as if it were a game,
like their children not fleeing but playing,
the two to them the same,
not trying to hide
but waiting in the park until
the light outside has died
and a blast bursts to bits their darkened doorsill.

4.
A Parisian lady's lace kerchief,
a dribble of sweat dripping off
an old priest's ear, bells in churches,

a flic's shades tinted the green of
a budding leaf, a chip of jade,
girls' hands unfolding like petals made
in China or Japan,
blooming, tightening into bud again,
small delicate hands that try
to hold a white orchid out to peace
or, in prayer, to a milk white anise
butterfly.

5.
Say the strangeness of any birth is
a sapphire in a chalice
a king, to rule,
must drink from, Versailles, Rouen,
the liquid blue of a sky
condensed to a jewel.
Where have you been,
boy, that led you here to die,
where you cannot freely think?
Your train is late,
past due in Vienna. The date
on your passport is no guarantee.
You're not the boy you might have been,
sneaking past guards who don't see
you trek through Turkey to a new royalty,
a caliphate to win.

6.
A double agent, fate,
mole, double crosser,
who doesn't ask for a fee,
who'd never rate
a mention in history,
like a poser
who cannot work alone,
a man of faith, heart of stone,
compiler of lists,

statistics,
in an old desert fortress.
He's fine, looks grand in his black
robes, flowing like fancy dress
in the West, looking to the night
to come,
as he taunts his fright-
ened captives on a site
destroyed like a wartime plaza in
Berlin,
in Rome.

7.
A fight for Baghdad,
cold as the face on his passport.
Outside a tent, flames
and smoke.
Another page torn from a report
that blames
the Jews. Each sheet elevates,
rises like a body, a cloak,
a bisht of an iman.
Sand
is the circle of retreat, the slow
grueling pace of soldiers go-
ing back to Amman,
the bombed streets of Homs,
the rubble of heretic minarets and domes.

8.
Thugs in New York streets,
subways, a report in the *Times*
that repeats,
the fear, the situation dire,
hopeless, with no justice or mercy
to appeal to, no conscience free,
no courtroom to go to.
All there is to know,

surveying the universe,
the cosmos,
is that what comes after is worse
than what's been before,
loss,
like the past, best forgotten,
but impossible
to, beheadings, massacres unforgiven,
unforgivable.

9.
Each tick-tock
or chime of a clock
races toward a midnight
that wanderers might
know, those who
have roamed,
left their rooms,
been to Barcelona, Kyoto,
the Maghreb, Sainte Reine de
Bretagne, Nairobi,
Delhi, Damascus, Istanbul
who have brought home
photographs, memories,
told anecdotes of how their lives grew more full
richer, more deep, spiritual, related stories
of how travel changed them,
the course
of their lives, for better, for worse.

10.
Books, music, poetry are more
holy when found in terror,
in wandering, quitting home, persuaded by a man
in a long black robe
to despise reason,
to go on a journey
of many victories won.

        Yet he's unsatisfied
by the miracle of killing
and so dies, who'd already died
in a paroxysm
of desert air, the willing
sacrifice,
the martyr
the West has made of him,
sending him to paradise
and themselves to hell, the fire
God's assigned them,
          the crusaders' desire
to destroy Islam
like fanatics of a blasphemous schism,
the flames they must aspire
to because of their terror
of his terror,
his dar-
ing, unshar-
able violence,
the mad sense
of deliberate horror.

11.
There's no end to it.
The war begins again today,
although it's never quit.

Mother of men,
mother of mercy,
compassion,
your wayward children are in danger
once more, now as forever,
the enemy at the door.

                    See
the sand blow in their faces,
choking them. Bring water,

show your rivers, lakes, oceans to them,
wash their eyes clean, enlighten
them who frighten
their God. Be kind
even to the sun-blinded,
the hawk-minded of the desert places
the heart must feed on.

                    Bestow
your love, show
them death must not win
over the endless nightly stories you tell,
the fantasy
that all might be well
some day, hell
denied by
you, your tales that undo
history—

you,
Mary,
Guanyin,
fearful, sad
Scheherazade.

Eight Voices after the War

1. Kathleen Ferrier

Her voice is an underworld. It is the soul's
descent. There's an umber color to it or a red
like the last embers from a fire that glows
in the dark. Perhaps she is singing for the dead
more than the living, for fall as much as spring.
Joy blossoms when, after wars, the earth is revived,
but she is bidding the world an early goodbye,
not wanting to leave it just when happiness's arrived
like an unexpected friend. She mustn't cry.
There's good that's left, and a singer's never alone.
She has her voice, her art. But only it can know
where she must travel. She feels a splintering, like a bone
breaking inside her. Her heart's weighed down by stone.
She's often cold. When she sings of forever, it's snow
on a river with no bridge to cross it, nowhere to go.

2. Elisabeth Schwarzkopf

She won't let the photographer film her. She's nearly ninety.
It would be unfair to her public to let them see her
when she is no longer a beauty. Severity
must be part of art, the need to deter a listener
from confusing what he sees on stage with what he hears.
There's been too much gossip, mean-spirited aspersions
about how she behaved in Germany during those years.
She was young, no Marschallin but poor. Conversions
came easily to her. Call it ambition. But listen.
When she sings, don't you notice something strange?
You're returning to a world you thought time had forbidden
you. Don't you feel as if you've gone home to where
you've never been, to some past where you might change
into what you've always wanted to be but did not dare?
Aren't you breathing a foreign air? And, if you feel sad,
think of what art could have made of the life you never had.

3. Maria Callas

Nothing is possible for her anymore. The gods
have abandoned her. Where's tragedy? All
is sorrow, boredom, grief. Each dull day plods
like an old Greek in a ripped black shawl.
Her rooms are full of expensive things, Chinese
jars, silk curtains, hand woven rugs, portraits of her.
Meaningless. She doesn't belong alone. Please,
she says, restore what's been lost. Hera, Demeter,
take me back to my mountain, to the olive grove
where goddesses dwell, the smell of fruit ripening
in the sun. To the temple, to the stage I love.
Teach me how to live again. How to sing
once more. Let me be passionate. Thrill to the din
of applause. *Io sono Medea.* I kill my children.

4. Dietrich Fischer-Dieskau

A great storm releases the Dutchman. Weary of the sea,
a singer is a mariner, too, praying for the tempest
to end. He's tired of torment, troubled by his memory
of battles. If he could find his love, he would rest.
Say she is Senta, dreaming, singing at her loom
where she is weaving a song of an ocean-tossed,
wind-battered man. Suddenly he stands in her room.
But his voice is doomed to wander, to feel lost
until the nightmare ends and a better world begins.
His own murdered his brother. His home was destroyed.
The horrors of the Russian front, his country's sins
haunt him wherever he performs. In Italy, he's employed
by Americans to entertain their prisoners of war,
his voice a just healed wound, a beautiful sad scar.

5. Hugues Cuenod

A voice *pour les entre-deux-guerres*, for Monteverdi
sing alongs at the *Princesse*'s salon, American
sewing machine heiress. A voice created for *mélodies*
and *lieder*, a sweet comprimario voice that began
as a boy soprano and stayed small as a piccolo,
with a bright, high vibrato. Think of sunlight off a man's silk
tie or wisps of floating mist fast vanishing below
the snow line of a Swiss valley or the difference between milk
and cream. Delightful filigree, ornaments. A stream
from a glacier. An old silver spoon. An ancient gold
plate Madame would serve *macarons* on. A dream
of his dying like Socrate, platonically, hemlock cold
at the end. At one hundred and five, Hugues Cuenod
marries his husband. He toasts him with high proof pernod.

6. Giuseppe di Stefano

Impoverished son of a carboniere, soldier in the war,
briefly a pupil of Cuenod, he struts with a tenor's
passion, a gondolier's style. His technique's far
from perfect, a young fighter's not an old warrior's
skill in him. But he always wins, is afterwards the braggart,
cheerfully smirking. Floria, don't give him the bum's
rush. He's seen your brush dew wet. Your heart
enjoys his wooing. Why care how quickly he comes?
He's impetuous in his singing, too. Like a Sicilian melon,
his butt is firm and musky as cypress. Why delay?
His voice is a silvery wave on the Mediterranean.
No matter that everyone's dead at the end of the play,
it's the ardency, speed, you live by that sings. Old, di Stefano
is beaten in the tropics. Death finds him to be untypically slow.

7. Franco Corelli

Rock Hudson's good looks, screen idol clichés befitting
him as no other singer then, his voice a trumpet
celebrating a hero, Manrico fighting, Radames setting
off to war. His high-C-maddened fans would let
Don Alvaro's or Calaf's or Rodolfo's last as long
as he could hold them before they'd applaud, disrupt-
ing the music with their bravos. Gymnastics, not song,
rivals' claques would grumble and rudely interrupt
him with booing and catcalls. Corelli is afraid.
The public scares him. His voice is at the whim
of their passions. The stage terrifies him. Has he stayed
on too long? Why won't he quit before they leave him?
They don't understand. At every performance, he
must surmount fearsome heights to be a Corelli.

8. Zinka Milanov

"Madame Milanov," I say to her backstage,
after her recital, two of her recordings in my hands
for her to sign. She does so gladly on the first page
of the *Trovatore* libretto. I think she understands
my pleasure. She inscribes the inside of the box
that holds the *Cavalleria* LP's with an even grander
flourish of her 'Z', like the curl in the tail of a fox
or a curlicue question mark. "You're a quick learner,"
she says to me, patting me on the head. I'm fifteen.
"So wise to love the opera." I shake the pianist's
hand, her brother, who played as an interlude the scene
Debussy wrote of the sea-sunken cathedral. He insists
it was nothing when I compliment him. Rusalka's
"Song to the Moon" was the last aria Milanov would sing
that evening, floating her famous high pianissimos
through the hall as if to me, my world, just beginning.

After a Schwarzwald Legend

The wild, deserted children, the sun-
less ones who hide in Black Mountain,
bring me gifts they've found, a triggerless gun,
a wheelless cart, a shirt with a bloodstain

on it, broken books, bread too old
to eat, limp flowers, a watch that won't run.
They say, "Your birthday's over. Though it's cold
where we live, come, have more fun

with us. You're not happy anyway."
So I go with them, not the only one
they've led astray through woods to play
with them, unguided by the sun

setting far west of Black Mountain.
The wolves know what's to be done.
The owls. The bats. The moths. The rain.
No rest. No rest at night for everyone,

no sleep to be had in their deep caves,
where I'm beset by waking dreams,
the boy I was who knows and saves
me, who has taken me where water streams,

but no light gleams, the trees too thick
to let in the sun, but berries and nuts
are plentiful, for toys a round stone, a stick
like a foil, snail slick or oak sap for cuts,

windstorms for music. Though the moon's dun
colored, the stars invisible, why shun
my friends? They've won. I've no cause to run.
I'm one of them now, the free, the sun-

less. I dwell in darkness, darkness in me,
the Black Forest, imagination,
the woodland of poetry
where children are born to abandon.

The Not inside You

"The only cure for loneliness is solitude."
Marianne Moore

1.
A boy's image is imprisoned in the glass of a window.
Could he release his reflection if he chose to, his face
on a rainy summer day sixty or more years ago?
He's gazing out at his father's soggy lawn. The lace
curtains in the living room are drawn back. The birds
are sopping, perched on drooping limbs. Worms–
pink, gray–are flailing on the walkway. A maid's words
are no comfort to him. There are lessons a boy learns
from bad weather. The games she suggests he play
he cannot win or lose. The lamp before him illuminates
his face on the window, flickering like a flame. Today,
as he stares at the boy, sad without any playmates,
he can't recall if he wanted in or out. Did he see
his fate in the glass, trapped, happy to be solitary?

2.
There's a strange, yet familiar pain in his gut, odd
new rumblings, his dried-up, blotched skin more wrinkled
this morning. It's not wrong, just unwise to blame God
for age's sorrows, the worrisome, ugly, crinkled
look on his face, the dizziness he feels when he
stands up too quickly, the slowing of his pace,
the names he can't remember, what he can't see
even with his glasses on. A sense of disgrace
is his country now, not belonging anywhere,
to anyone in the terror his mother left for a face,
the mask she wore after her death, in the final
breath his father took, the sudden exhaling of air
as he died. Paradise must be a lonely place.
So much pain to justify. All he's refused to call.

3.
He knows nothing of gods. The mountain's quiet. Magic
has fled the earth or was expelled alongside tragedy.
He's bored. Even trees dwell in solitude. He's sick
of pretending the old myths are true. You see
before you an agèd Greek man wearing a worn
black shawl, mourning for the islands he's lost.
He doesn't belong here or deserve the city's scorn
and its chastisements. Let him return to his coast,
his mountain top, where the sun makes the smell
of lemons pervade the heat, to the god-dwelling temple,
the theater he loved, to make believe, to his sin-
less, sensual world of sand and sea. Tell
him there's a way to restore the ancient simple
things, that he's not landless, homeless, without kin.

4.
He sings a song of drowning out of men's sight,
a wrecked ship in its music, wind blown, hawk's cry,
broken shells, bones sinking in sand, a night
when sleepers awake in fear, their dreams not a lie
but a foreboding, plovers scattering before
hill-high waves, heavy as mud slides. Melodies
roll in, retreat, repeat, break on the shore,
mingling words, harmonies, rhythms, keys,
intoning a requiem icy water keeps to itself:
a drone, the moaning of a tempest long after
it's gone, the storm sea-weary like a mariner,
wind-battered, who swims for dry land. The shelf
where he stands at low tide tolls with the laughter
of crewmen mocking him, derelict lonesome sailor.

5.
He wanders underground, a cold world, his soul
its rock face, umber, lead-flecked, mouldering,
its coal mined out. Above, on earth, is the hole
he fell through. He descends deeper, ring after ring.
His eye is a small round black spot for a snake

to hide in. He is looking for his dearest friend
who left before him. How long death seems to take.
They'd climbed up snow-capped peaks, down valleys, pretend-
ing it might last, years ago, out of some need
to explore a strange country, the cold world apart
from all they'd known where icicles on trees splinter,
scatter like bones, thoughts drift like a solitary reed
down a stream until it freezes over and the heart
turns to ice. It is death to separate. It is zero winter.

6.
A priest jogs on a dusty path in ancient plains
through forests, past corn fields, barns. He is running
so fast because love is outpacing him, like rains
that fall ahead of him and move on, drenching
only others. He has preached God is the Not
inside you all humanity shares. He runs and runs
because this is Poland and the dirt underfoot is the rot
of its years, its centuries of bloodshed and persecutions.
Let him lie on a bed in a room with no source of light.
See how brightly it's lit. He's just had sex with a boy
who will leave him for seminary. God is the sight
of a body you love lying beside you, a pleasure, joy
that's forbidden, like a priest, unmarried, husband
to no one, in love with a boy in the solitude of Poland.

Three Prayers

1.
The sea consecrates the sky. Light seeps into caves
and clings. It's hot. There are no shadows. Crows
rip into plastic bags of rotting food. One braves

a garbage can, strews waste on streets. Wind blows
it onto the beach. Say I am a monk sitting on
a hill overlooking a gorge in which a river flows

over rocks. He sips rice wine. He hears the battle's won
and chants an old poem about a drunken moon.
A white crane flies over a mulberry tree, a son

of the sky or a Buddha. A lark, a swallow, a loon
pass overhead. Women are threshing in the valley.
Can dawn come too late for them or dusk too soon?
The hills are burning. He prays to a languid noon.

2.
How I need you green, like a night without
dreaming, as I need thoughts of home where
I'd play hide and seek and yell and shout

and run wild in the woods and meadows where,
a small boy after the war was won, I
was safe in shadows. How I need dawn's air,

the smell of apples' blossoming, the dew I lie
on like a bed, the gentle grasses, their
timelessness, the laughter and childlike sigh

of the wind blowing through them, alone, no care
in the world, no worries, as if other children
were playing with me, each of us a pair,
revealing our secrets, our pain, the prayers we share.

3.
The sun is on fire. It burns the pine all summer,
its light proof of the life to come. Or maybe not.
My doubt is rain on a barn roof, whose scatter

shot sound, like rumbling thunder, relieves a hot
day. My life is not yet done. My mind's a boy,
sometimes a child, a happiness old age forgot

or forgets, a kid's meandering down rows of corn,
not yet grown to his size, each stalk like a toy
to play with, staying up nights when stars torn

from the sky fall close by, meaning to bring
him news. The end will come like a star at dawn
that in its descent is revelation, the sense of everything:

the smell of boxwood, burning leaves, a just mowed lawn,
the taste of lemon cakes, apples, honeyed almonds,
the sight of a heron fishing in a lake, a swan

resting in rushes, untroubled by storms, fern fronds,
hail crackling on an asphalt road, summer breezes,
the mist off shallow streams, frogs croaking in ponds.

All these that come back to me, whatever seizes
my senses still, let them be born in me again,
willows, dogwood, roses, any memory that teases

me into belief in a holiness only earth can sustain,
an ocean, its waves rushing to shore, that glories
in prayer as a bird in flight does, or falling rain,
or moonlight shining through an icy windowpane.

Thirteen Fragments from a Lost Gospel

1.
The dawn's winter-clear. The ocean's white water,
wind-blown, is light as snow. On a dune,
a statue hewn
from oak, in his glistening wet suit, a surfer

checks out the currents, which way the waves break,
the sea's rhythms,
its beat, listens
as its waves smash onto shore, flow back, lake-

like lapping the sand, black from tar or the cinders
from bonfires. To catch a wave's ride
is to be alive, to abide
in sea's song, what Odysseus heard lashed to timbers.

2.
An angel flies down to warn: Herod's on a rampage,
slaughtering new born
sons torn
from their mothers' breasts, all those your child's age.

Take flight to Egypt. Reverse the exodus to
be free. Let one
be saved. Like stone,
the tyrant's heart. Say I am the dark spirit who

weeps even as he watches your family flee
to Saïs, find refuge, bed,
where sand, water wed,
an oasis from pain, from Rachel's rage against savagery.

3.
Compassionate Lady. Mary. Mother. Quan Yin.
You see your son weave
from rose stems and grieve
at the little crown he makes. It must begin

somehow. He pricks his finger on a thorn.
It bleeds. What good does it do
to plead with him? He must be true
to his innocence. How can he be careful? Like a boy born

a bleeder, he sees you follow him everywhere.
His thumb is red. You suck
the wound clean. What luck
is in blood that tastes like wine to him, to you despair?

4.
A boat with a single sail slides across
the Sea of Galilee. Its waters part
to a late dawn light. His heart
longs for the further shore, the rushes the waves toss.

An ox heaves itself awake. In search of dew,
food, a ram bounds
from rock to rock. Sounds
of snakes, lizards licking desolation from the sand. Who

is the prophet's new follower? The Jordan's cold. Locusts
fly over head, rattle
like palms, a far-off battle.
For him, the reeds divide. A wind rises and gusts.

5.
Unclean, twelve years a bleeder, a woman
presses toward him, ever nearer.
The mob recoils. Dearer
to him than they, she trembles to touch his cloak. Her plan

is plain to him. A seamstress when young, she knows
and trusts the virtues women
sew in clothes, coarsely woven
like his. Which somehow still adorn him, a light that glows

from the man before whom she cowers, who calls
her daughter, her gushing blood
dried by metonymy, hood
or sash or hem from which his power falls.

6.
A mountain top, sun-dazzled. A song of sorts,
a fugue perhaps or the beat
on deer skin drums. In the heat,
wailing, black-clad women, once consorts

of Bacchus, toss seeds on their children's graves, tearing
their hair. In the Negev,
in Compostela, Kiev
holy men chant it. Sun-quickened birds sing

it at noon. A violinist plays its Bach-like tune.
A tenor hits a high C
while a little girl, a century
dust, gathering nuts, hums it to the moon.

7.
Lost, stolen—the old man can no longer remember—
but gone, impoverishing
him for good, the ruby ring
cut like glass to form an oval window his master

could peer through so that the day Gaius slit his veins
the wine-soaked, happy
Brundisium he could see
through his stone was red as the bowl his blood still stains.

A slave, he squats in a fig grove. His stools stink
and steam. Figs cramp
his guts. The ground's damp.
Spirit birds fly near the moon whose light must sink

each night, unweaving more threads from his threadbare life,
his only shelter a cave,
no use except to save
him from the wind, where the dead sleep, strife-

ridden. Their cries, screams, ruin his peace. Then: "Take.
Eat. Loaves. Fishes."
Miracles. Wishes
come true. "Do not hide your faces. For my sake,

strip off your sackcloth. No longer deceive your Lord.
Wear new clothes. Love
your neighbor above
yourself, you who will leave me one by one, my adored,

my beloved." Is the white sliver on his finger a chunk
of a tooth from an ivory
comb or a fish bone? He's as weary
as his master at his last meal, drinking to get drunk.

However much the crowd devours, the basket never
empties. He grabs more food
than he could eat. It'll be good
for later. Naked, no loincloth, his arms no thicker

than its thinnest roots, a boy leans against an oak
tree god. Careful not
to touch his sores, the rot
on his nose, the old man opens his pouch. "Don't choke

on the bone. Eat this bread instead, soaked soft
in wine I can easily
find more of. See.
The crowd is leaving. Maybe I mocked him, scoffed

at his tricks. Well, to hell with the old ways and politics,"
the old man says to the boy.
"The world'll be ours to enjoy
without Roman soldiers and their crucifix."

8.
The battering rams keep pounding. The enemy's regrouping.
I didn't mean to leave you.
Tell me, Peter. Is it true,
the pursuit over? But I can hear the swords. What thing

is death? Why will they murder him? Or is it
his gift to the birthday of time?
I was born in swamps, in the slime
left from paradise. Tonight the sky is smokeless, lit

with stars. This message I send you is a sure sign
of spring, a leaf from a tree.
I could not live, could not be
without you, Jerusalem, no longer mine.

9.
A green fire burns the earth. Gusts of wind
blow south from an icy
north, stingingly,
withering blossoms. The fig the boy eats is the kind

that lasts best. Scattered about the olive grove,
men lie on the ground,
sleeping. There's the sound
of soldiers surmounting the hill. What did he do? "Love,"

he'd said. Roman torches drip blood-red cinders,
sparks. They wake,
scared, take
off. The boy's linen cloth falls. Naked, he flees like his followers.

10.
Pilate's gardens are jeweled like fall in Gaul
where in winter his men
wore fur and hide, stolen
from the beast hordes they put to the sword, the tall

northern warriors, their woods thick with trees
as Nile banks with reeds.
Great Rome sows seeds
of confusion. Tomorrow, he crucifies in threes.

Death will wait patiently for them, loyal as a soldier.
He likes to watch the eyes
of the crucified. The one who dies
scanning the sky for signs of hawks dies years older.

11.
Beside himself, accuser and accused. Do not say
en masse people many
no lists there are not any
for the body-strewn rice fields the locked barns hay

cattle women men children burning alike
start with your own
the earth is sown
with them God near infinitely far noose spike

rack lost for words he must quote a psalm
forsaken into pain
the cross's stain
he bleeds away or do we not breathe at all

12.
Dressed in blinding white, a young man, angel,
apparition, frightens three
women who cannot see
him for the light. And yet, soon after, they will tell

the others whom they saw, the desolate men
gathered in a room
dark as the tomb
they've buried him in. It was no crime, no sin,

for them to lie, if that is what the women did. Light
often tricks the eye,
turns fact to fable. Did he die?
Truth writes in cipher ink on paper as white.

13.
Lovers of gardens, lovers of men, each time
you die shine brighter
each time. Whiter and whiter,
the waves this Christmas morning, the dawn a rhyme

from the past, the surprise or the expected gift.
Atticus and I stand
where we stood, hand
in hand, last year. A flock of gulls lift

off the beach as they do time after time, season
after season, a brilliant light
gleaming from their feathers, bright
as the sun on new snow, shining for no reason.

Fourteen Stations of the Cross (1)

1.
The sun's pale,
flat above
a broken horizon,

rising, sail-
ing out of
dark. Its swiftly blazon-

ing thick light,
rain-, mist-like
gray, turns flaming yellow.

Dying night
shadows strike
incisive strokes below

the hills, trees'
calligraphy
brushed the ancient ways,

as ink frees
hands to see
its clarity is day's.

2.
In the park,
October
summer burns the leaves

and grass dark
as amber
sap or bark, deceives

the eye with
its brightness,
the light flaked like rust.

For the fifth
day, it's press-
ing down on air, dust-

like to breathe,
the body
oppressed by its bril-

liance, its seeth-
ing, sheer white
sky by noon, the shrill-

ness of it,
sublimity
nearly unbearable

the way lit
not to see
but be incredible.

3.
Newman's *Four-*
teen Stations
of the Cross, in a room

built just for
them. The Son's
not here, his silence tomb-

struck. Why, no
more than black,
white, unprimed canvas,

strokes made so
by the rack
of geometry, by absence,

the story
vanished, lost
to history, the myth

fantasy
or a ghost
haunting daily with

its death, the
tragedy
within sublimity;

why, for me,
here to see
unseen things, unrea-

sonable
to my mind,
do I, as long ago

in a fable
I'd heard, find
what I could never know

but believe
I have seen
through these abstractions,

can perceive,
can find mean-
ings, intimations, horizons

beyond the
visible,
mournful Achilles

by the sea
unable
to fight, his sword, greaves

by his side
already dead
as prophesied, no

mortal, hid-
ing, as said
of Christ crucified, to

come again,
glorified;
why, in these paintings,

stroke and stain,
simplified,
risible plain things

easy to mock,
portentous
nothings, nonsense; why do

I take stock,
momentous
reckonings of you,

me, say I
see while there
staring intently

God, that lie,
real, unfair
as in all tragedy

he must be,
the suffering
these paintings are, how today,

most strangely,
with the sting
of time, they show the way

of the cross
to the light
at the end of it,

fateful loss,
the bare white
entombment, the spirit?

4.
The walk back
wet, muggy,
the doubt that returns,

the void, lack,
loss only,
nothing, what one learns

by looking,
reality
too visible maybe,

everything
so simply
what it is, the sea,

the sun blank
white at noon,
its light piercingly hot,

the rot, rank,
of raccoon
and rat, nothing not

sure, the path
underfoot,
the canopy, the birds

or the wrath
to come, route
and way, his last words

death, empti-
ness, what New-
man saw, his forsakenness,

Jesus's plea,
sabachthani,
the forgiving bless-

ing that si-
lence can be,
the absolute's muted Yes.

Fourteen Stations of the Cross (2)

1. Jesus is Condemned to Death

The future is an absolute, the law's strictest law,
the black pit inside you, the gap in time,
the father, long dead and buried, you think you saw
coming at you in the attic with a knife in his hand.

2. Jesus Carries His Cross

Who carries the burden of his own death bears
the weight of everything. Old woman, lying in
your sick room, this night, so late, reflects your fears.
Strange eyes in the mirror shed tears like yours.

3. Jesus Falls for the First Time

The blue glacier's dazzling seen from over head,
the ledge you stand on less than two yards wide.
Tempted by an abyss like the comforts of bed,
you slip into the cold descent of night.

4. Jesus Meets His Mother

The olive grove, cedar forest he played in as a child,
the hilltop garden with its hidden healing stream,
the name you gave him before he was born, the wild
one you never used, denying it to him until now.

5. Simon of Cyrene Helps Jesus Carry the Cross

Pick him up in your arms. Hold him tightly like
a mother, a lover, the beaten body you embrace
the weight of terror that it carries. You try to strike
back at his pain, the gravity your muscles strain against.

6. Veronica Wipes the Face of Jesus

An old bum limps. His foot's badly swollen. His collar's
blood-stained, his beard spittle-gray. He rages
in tongues, begs for mercy, food, booze, a few dollars.
HIs handkerchief is filthy. He wipes the sweat off his brow.

7. Jesus Falls the Second Time

A girl says, "I thought I was all right until
that morning I stumbled down the stairs. Or said
I'd tripped. I lied. I knew better. I'm ill
and will keep on falling like that, like him, forever."

8. Jesus Meets the Women of Jerusalem

The women of the plaza weep. You know well what city
this is. Name any other you might care to that war
has sacked. Pity the mothers of the disappeared who'd pity
you more if you brought back their daughters and sons.

9. Jesus Falls for the Third Time

So weak the day, it collapses, unassisted, on its own
like a miracle that didn't work. Trickster,
healer, weak in arm and leg, you're known
by the rain you promised to bring, by its springtime falling.

10. Jesus Is Stripped of His Garments

Nakedness is the sun become human. It blinds you if
you stare at it too long. Like goodness. Or the moon,
undone by time, daily waning, no dif-
ferent from what it was at its birth, ashamed of dying.

11. Jesus Is Nailed to the Cross

The wordlessness of pain, its notorious silence,
the blank nothing of suffering, what art aspires to,
what's not possible to say, the mute absence
of God, what compassion fails at, wounded by its failure.

12. Jesus Dies

Try to imagine it. Try to imagine your oblivion.
Yet it's you imagining it, you standing in the blank
nothing, the dark, hearing, "It's too late, my son,
my only begotten, for the life I forgot to give you."

13. The Deposition

Down. Down. Take it all down. All
of it. You're leaving town. You're moving somewhere
else. Carry what you can in your arms. Call
it enough: underclothes, a lock of his hair, photographs.

14. The Entombment

On winter nights in New Hampshire, in northern gloom,
by full moon's reflection the snow on pastures
shines brighter than by day. In a limestone tomb,
in Jerusalem, death glows like moon on whitest snow.

The Light That Lasts Past Light's Decay

I. An Embarkation and Stanzas Set to Rhymes by Alice Elgar

1.
No ships, no boats dock here to let off, take
on passengers or cargo. The pier's pilings rise
from fog-thick mist. At night, the Pacific tries
to hide its killer currents. The lights look fake,
too incandescent, like ghosts that glow within.
They show you to pier's end where nothing waits
except the dark that hints of sailors' fates,
lost, drowned at sea. So old stories begin.
Of voyaging. Of journeying between two worlds.
Piers are bridges to nowhere. Walk out. Peer deep
into water. Then turn around. As if asleep,
you're dreaming a dream you must repeat, like words
of a prayer. *I thought I was to meet him here.*
I've waited all night. Why doesn't his ship appear?

2.
Come, Love. Hold my hand.
A pier's more sure than land.
Since nothing ours may stand,

walk out. The waves beat fast,
cities fall, bombs blast,
fire rages. Earth cannot last.

Walk to the end with me. I say,
"Such mist is yesterday, today.
It burns away. Why stay?"

And you. You stare into the night
as if it gave delight
like a ship on its way to harbor.

II. Promontory and a Poem Set to Rhymes by Housman

1.
Rocks, many a black jagged promontory
jutting haphazardly into the sea,
shrouded, gauzy, the same uncolor gray
as the sky. No signs of life. Neither night nor day,
or both, like a memory I'm trying to forget
of someone I've loved and lost and regret
not having loved enough before nothing's left
but to let grief be. The world is also bereft,
empty, like a chill in the night that makes
me shudder, shining through an icy Pacific.
The earth stripped, denuded to rocks, sea, sky
is no consolation even if sorrow is what it takes
for me to see beyond myself. The world is sick.
It hurts like an innocent child. The light says why.

2.
She is ill. She is hurting. Unknown, the number
of her days ahead. She will not return again.
Too soon her loss cries out in me, my 'slumber,'
romantic word, lost to me, romantic as 'pain.'

No bird, no dog, no man, no 'you' is just a thing.
A soul inhabits all that lives. To be
is to be with God, abdicated, throneless, no king,
no ruler, but whatever descends to you or me

in an angel's guise, pentecostal, burning,
like my dog barking at a crow taking off in flight
with no hope of catching it or of its returning
and my chasing after her, leashless, all night.

III. The Rocks and a Poem Set to an Acrostic on 'Rachmaninoff'

1.

It is low tide. Wide beach. The shallow water
ripples like a lake, windy,
night-stricken. No world exists other
than this: sky, clouds, three gulls, rocks, sea.
Alleluia.

The sun is setting in the V of a boulder
as if between mountains in a valley
long bare of trees, craggy, its light colder
than the moon's seas. Let night be.
Alleluia.

These rocks are blacker than night,
darker than men's fears. As if free,
more stunning than sunlight,
warningly, they rise out of the sea.
Alleluia.

Let scattered clouds sleep out each night
upon the breasts of massive
matter. It is their right
that men should die and stones still live.
Alleluia.

Bleak, their message, their eternal peace,
their quietude, their stone dark
shadows that know no release
from material tragedy, its stark
alleluia.

2.

Rocks rise out of water as in a Zen garden. What made them
able to be so ritually placed exactly there? Chance or artistry? No
clocks, computers, no geometry can make more
habitable the world into which all things are thrown. Yet order

mocks also, like a dictator smitten with strictness who stands
astride the world, laughing at its folly, its demand to be told.
No hands arranged these rocks, beautifully here, just barely
inside an ebbing tide. Each boulder could be a character in a
Noh play, the sunset its painted pine backdrop or brushed cipher
O. Rocks' shadows are ink-soaked calligraphic black. Can souls be
fortified, immortalized by stone? Design, happenstance, neither is
friend or foe. No more is God. Rocks rise out of water as in a Zen
      garden.

IV. A Tree on a California Hill and a Poem Beginning with a Phrase
from Horace

1.
A lonely tree, ancient, wind-tormented, reaching
toward earth, its bushy limbs, spiked, jagged
like uprooted roots, pointing, admonishing, beseeching–
Lear on the heath, abandoned, worn, haggard,
shaking his bony fingers in rage, in fury
against the sky, the heavens, the tragedy
of a world electrified, exposing the wrath inside,
its killer lightning. The hills slope like thighs, ass seen
by a lover, the grass smooth as mats of hair,
as sweaty skin, glistening. The tree has not died
yet. Though winds have bent it, it is not keen
like a sick wolf to crawl into its mother's lair,
drawn there by seeds' smells and loamy earth,
broken by storms it's known as a god since birth.

2.
Immortalia ne speres. No matter. A growing boy
still is thrilled by late August thunderstorms
that break each afternoon, the clouds' forms,
signs shifting so quickly fresh patterns destroy
the old before he can read them. Billowing,
black, they conquer a retreating sky. No blue,
no white, no sun: the old, dull world's made new.

92

He waits for the first bolt, attack of lightning,
then counts the seconds until the thunder cracks.
An ancient pine stands in his backyard, ninety feet
high, the tallest tree on a long, wooded street.
When lightning hits, he is soaked to the bone. It wracks
the pine, igniting it. The smoke, the taste of resin
as it burns fill him with joy for no earthly reason.

V. Two Poems Set to the Same Rhymes

1. The Roar of Verdi's *Il Trovatore*

Her forbidden lover wanders through the night
like a shade she cannot see and barely hear,
his voice far off and melodious, palely clear,
like the song of an itinerant ghost that's scarily white.

As he waits to fight, smoke dirties the sky,
hides him from her sight. He wears it like a mantle,
his gypsy face blackened by soot, like the kettle
in which his mother cooks, the fire he's sworn by.

Emptiness, moon, true father of the brother
the witch incinerated in her pyre, look down, see
how we die, you, like the sun, enemy
of the darkness you shine through like a lover,

show what's left when the conflagration's done, the last son
burned alive, after hate's spent, after Armageddon.

2. The Silence of a Photograph

Slate black, slate gray, silvery, whether night
or day impossible to say, nothing to hear,
nothing to say except nothing made clear,
no writing on the slate, no scrawls or marks, chalk white.

No tides, no waves, the sea is darker than the sky.
No sun, moon, stars. The world wears a mantle,
a flat back drop black as a pot or kettle,
the fire burned out, only an ashen light to see by.

As if the aftermath of time were your lost brother,
your sister, the twin, the double through whom you see
death face to face and know it is not your enemy
but, as the ballads used to say, your demon lover.

A man stands knee deep, shadow black, sees God's son
in sea's, sky's silence, Jesu, done with Armageddon.

VI. Two Pastoral Poems, Their Rhymes Reversed

1.
Clouds, mountains, trees are mirrored by the lake,
but not reversed, inverted to trees, mountains, clouds.
The water reflects a darker scene, waves that break
like an avalanche, a tsunami that astounds
with its power. What is coming is worse than bad weather.
Apocalypse. Skies that appear to threaten no harm,
that over hills look like a winter storm,
are seen on a Marin lake to hide a nether
world. Hills, grass, tree groves welcome the rain,
but look below. Waves churn up the stain
that taints all things. The fall. The lake is to blame,
clouds, hills, trees seen through the soul, the same
soul as yours in a mirror. Peer deep. Let it tell
you why the earth as it is was the paradise that fell.

2.
What if God had caught the earth in his arms as it fell?
Embraced us, too? What stories of him would we tell?
Thirteen, a boy circles a lake in Marin, the same
lake he's been hiking for weeks, looking. Who'd blame
him? He longs to find him again, hunkering, a stain

like a mandala on his t-shirt, drenched by a warm rain,
cupping his hands. The kid's afraid of the nether
world, hell's pit, where bad boys go. A new storm
stirs behind the hills. The guy looks hungry. What harm
can it do? He gives him his sandwich. The weather
is changing to spring. The stranger winks, astounds
the boy with his smile. The sun's about to break
through. He strips, swims away. Light as light, clouds,
hills, trees float like him, airily on a dazzling lake.

VII. Normandy/Ocean Beach: A Double Sonnet

Nine thousand soldiers lay dead on Normandy beach.
Nine women, men stroll along the Pacific.
Their lives ground to sand like shells, coral, bones.
They build a bonfire circle out of flotsam from ships.
Hank died there, Leon, medics who took the breach.
Dave Sue June Steven Lou Michael Kay Lee Rick.
Mowed down from cement bunkers, gravestones.
They party, drink beers, eat burgers, corn chips.
On Tarawa, Anzio, Iwo, the sand as blood soaked.
Two minstrels, guitar players, sing to sundown.
Their silence in the tumult beforehand, the grief.
They sing trusting happiness to drive away death.
In the land craft, no one spoke, no one joked.
The sea is where they are free, not in a city or town.
Some found their way across, waited for relief.
They dance to the breakers till they're all out of breath.
The bodies looked drawn on sand in silhouette.
At twilight, each body is black as a silhouette.
Or like game caught at night in a trap or a net.
Reflected in tide pools, their shadows are wet.
So many bodies it took days to haul them away.
Nine friends strolling on wave-packed sand.
On Normandy, nine thousand soldiers dead.
Nine friends walk like shades on the Pacific strand.
How many people were killed elsewhere that day?

They will soon form a line, hand in hand.
The beach bled humanity. The channel turned red.
They dance to the waves. To the sky. They dance to the land.

VIII. *Il Tramonto* and a Poem Set to a Line and Rhymes by Shelley

1.
The sun is refulgent through a scrim of clouds.
It is the Lord's eye on the world, gazing down
upon an archipelago, on a small island town
where banished Greeks live, a world allowed
only by fantasy, inspired by a few craggy rocks,
blemished with guano, strange snail-like antennae,
that rise out of the sand and a mist beset sea.
Can imagination find sacred time, stop human clocks?
Sun, wind, waves, boulders, low fog forget
nothing. The Delian League is preparing for
war. Their rulers love their people who adore
their gods. Yet they'll lose. Ancient regret
laps like waves on Pacific rocks, memory's
outcroppings. Triremes clash in far flung seas.

2.
If madness 'tis to be unlike the world,

to take no comfort in sunset, in ocean air
so bracing to others, to find no pleasure in a ray
of sunlight falling on a crag of boulder, there

for a moment, then gone, I look the other way,
backward to the past, to its frowning countenance,
see history in whatever is before me, night or day

uncover in a lover's smile, a stranger's glance
a sign, a memory of men who have died–
as if to live my life in this world is to dance

with the dead in the one they miss. Wayside
paths are worth traveling, the future having passed
behind me. On this beach, five rocks abide

in a timeless world, like a plaster sculpture cast
in bronze. Though storms, tides, waves have rolled
over them for centuries, they endure, they last

unlike us, mad, not to be held by, kept in the fold
of

IX. Sun Moon and a Poem Set to Rhymes by Tennyson

1.
The light is as chillingly pure as Schubert's *Nacht
und Träume* sung by Elly Ameling (that "little
Dutch girl," Wustman called her), an icy, brittle
light, as if peering through frosted glass you're shocked
to discover how bright it is, how huge in the sky
is the space it occupies. Rivulets, fresh or salty,
flow into and out of the bay–land, not sea
on the far horizon. The place people go to die
is waiting nearby. Vision's confounded by what it sees:
sun moon clouds mist sand, glowing and cold.
Birds perch by water's edge, as if ready
to fly whenever they're told wherever they please,
like souls longing for the night when the old
light in its new Ra boat sets sail, God-steered and steady.

2.
Water. Light. There's no godlier a good.
  But my moon-soaked mind's not right, is ill
  with fantasies, unfettered by will.
Dreams stain my brain like sheets with blood.

At night, in bed, the shuffle of feet
  on staircase and rug. My lovers destroyed

before me walk out of the void
into my sleep. The time I've dreaded's complete.

"You are selfish," they say. "You are vain
  to want to live on and on, to desire
  life burn forever with youthful fire.
Eternity frees you. There's nothing to gain."

I wake to a light colder than anything
  I felt in the dark. It is early fall,
  the coast fogged in, the beach and all
the dunes soaked as after rain in spring.

The full moon is frozen, white. I
  watched it through the long night
  shine through my window. Its icy light
cracks at dawn with an icily inhuman cry.

X. Styx and a Poem Beginning *Laudate*

1.
Hymn hymn hymn. The sky, the unseen hills,
the ground below, the light. Creation. Windows.
Girders. Oh, Jonathan, the night refills
by heaven's right the streams, the bay. Rows
of floors are climbing. Where are you two staying?
Why are you tired of praying? More dawn than noon-
time scattered clouds. Lovers used to sing
in harmony. Donald. Steve. Jim. Too soon,
too quickly, all things change. Forgive sins?
When praise comes, the shock of it begins
anew. Why not confound what's here, the far
for near? High rises. The taller they are
the more they sway, I hear. Buildings are a river
like the Styx. Hymn hymn, Charon, praise-giver.

2.
Laudate, omnes gentes, laudate dominum.
Despite the ruins of time, despite history,
the crimes it's committed, the horrors yet to come,

despite cruelty, monstrous or petty,
despite the reality of horror, of suffering,
despite knowing that our fate is tragedy,

praise. Praise because it's absurd, nothing,
ridiculous, scandalous, senseless. Irrationally,
praise. Praise like a fool, an idiot singing

for no reason, without words or a tune. The sea
waits for you, the sky, the earth. Look about,
stare up, peer down. Death is a formality,

a ritual, an architecture that no one can doubt,
a mathematics, a geometry. Buildings greet
the minds that try to figure them out,

but, like people, they change even as they repeat
themselves to stand weightily floor upon floor.
So windows may look identical until the treat

of a shift in the light and the sky that is more
than a trick of sun or eye or a mere asymmetry
lets you see what you've been searching for,

a peek into heaven, a glimpse of glory.
The strictness of a building is its fury,
its rage against formlessness. Sun, wind, sea
tell a similar story. Light strikes a high rise. *Laudate.*

XI. The Jesus Tree and a Poem Set to a Line and End Words by Wordsworth

1.
At the foot of your son's tree, Mother, invisible,
you weep. The field in which it starkly stands
breaks like waves on sea-borne, wind-blown lands
that bear his weight and blood. There is trouble
in heaven. The light in the sky is a fire behind
its nervous trunk and limbs, anxious as a mind.
Spirit flows in wood fibre and sap. Muscle
and blood incarnate a soul. Can the visible
alone be real? Mother, Eva, Diane, Isabel,
Leona, Liv, the tree on which your son bleeds
is yours, is you. *Stella maris,* shine on your loss,
what must fall on sea and land as its fellows fell.
Teach us to pray trees like a rosary's beads,
to adore them like relics from the one true cross.

2.
Touch–for there is a spirit in the woods.
Surprisingly, as if unexpected, the end came.
I'd climbed Mount Tam. Now it is old age
that shocks, the vast view witnessed for an hour
or two from the summit, then, the holiday
over, the trek back down, the Marin woods gone
for more like a lifetime, the reason I came
across the bay to Phoenix Lake overpowered
by a desire to be lost in a forest I never forgot.
A little boy, no more than four or five, I'd been
allowed to roam there freely. Maybe it said,
"There's no need to get lost if you live as trees live."
I don't know. I became a city man and thought
an occasional trek up Tam was enough, to intrude
far back where trees, uprooted, crash and die.
Now, if I could, I'd return to the ancient stands, not from hope,
not according to necessity, Anaximander's thought,
but to smell the acrid pine resin bleeding, to be

young again, fearlessly lost in woods, not his,
not anyone's, the light filtered through needles a green
dark as lichen or moss, the rot and humus depth
enough for him as he rested and searched above
the canopy, beyond the sun, to find the spot
where his breath, the light came from, the source of desire
in trees, in him, his small boy's godward gaze.

XII. White on White and a Poem Set to a Sentence and a List of
Words from a Page by John Cage

1.
Black is eternal silence, Kandinsky wrote,
yellow the color of earth. But white is beginning,
the sound of the Ice Age, the first note
of a purified world, snow-covered, nothing.
Nothing. White on white. Malevich. The beauty
of silence, the void, absence. No history,
no memories, a clear day, as Stevens said
on his way to the bus. White, the color of the dead,
the no-self, *muga*. To discharge one's duty
on the battlefield, Suzuki observed, is a religious
act. Lamentation bears no fruit. The sword, not he
who wields it, kills. The self is a prodigious
madness. Abandon the will. War is a rite
of compassion. Self-sacrifice is the color white.

Retreat. Snow in the valleys, on the mountain's slopes,
the narrow ledges the soldiers must climb, descend
next to precipices. No going home, no hopes
left for them, blinded by night or by snow, the end
alone clearly in sight, their buddies' screams
in their ears as they fell to their deaths. What redeems
man is faith in Christ alone, Paul wrote, who
had seen his lord in a vision he knew must be true
because it blinded him. Who wrote nothing of Jesus
the man except that he died on the cross by self-

sacrifice to save us from sin, to free us
from ourselves. On a perilously slippery shelf
of a Korean mountain, my husband's father tried
to live by clinging to the shoe of a soldier who'd died.

What does the Buddha see, gazing inwardly
westward toward a nearly blinding light?
His statue seems to float. Think Jesus on the Sea
of Galilee walking on water, the miracle fright-
ening his followers. Buddhas of light, of water,
of reflection. His shadow in the pool is also
who he is. Ring of sand, of cloud, of horizon,
the circle of enlightenment. Abandon son, daughter,
father, mother, brother, Jesus demanded. Go
with him. The Buddha faces a setting sun
traveling west toward heaven, the Pure Land.
Say his name to light, tide, rock, sand.
Amida comes, transports you across the sea
to an eternity that is not, where not is purity.

2.

Earth's no escape from heaven.
A man, Gautama, knows nothing of love.
He laughs often, but knows little of mirth.
He pursues soldiers, thinks them heroic.
Good drink is the most he tastes of wonder.
A comfortable bed is the meaning of tranquility.
Then, one day, outside, he learns the fear
of death in a suppurating body, anger
in the marketplace where it lies, no sorrow
for it shown, no compassion, only disgust.
A beggar asks, Is there a glass of water?

The lecturer is warm. Is there a glass of water?
He is arguing that feelings such as love,
hate hinder men's attention. Mirth
is clarity. He laughs at those heroic
aspirations of a music that forgets the wonder

to be heard in sounds and noises. Tranquility
is to be found in chance, not choice. Fear
comes from clinging to one's will. Anger
also imprisons the mind. No will, no sorrow.
The self, egoism, is why men feel disgust.
Earth's no escape from heaven.

Earth's no escape from heaven.
Is this world our only home? Love,
tragedy are ours like skin and bone. Mirth
may follow grief like a satyr play. Heroic
ideals lead to wars. But is there not wonder
in some men's deeds, even if tranquillity
is elusive? I know there is much to fear,
death most of all. And, yes, to be is to sorrow.
Age corrupts the flesh. But must we feel disgust?
If a man thirsts, give him a glass of water,

friend, since Jesus, Buddha,
to our wonder, to their surprise,
in paradise are thirsty too.

Stone Altars

1.
The black rocks are for where the images fail,
for where the living lie buried
with the drowned among uncarved
stones. Flags are unfurled on ships once they sail

far from harbor or appear over the horizon,
piratical like those
you saw as boys
when they came for you, dark as these rocks. The sun,

luminescent, fills the sky with promise of return, the ground
of the sea bright as a mountain's
slope, the west sunset-lit like plains.
Beyond them, everything is silence, no sound

left in the world. Two gnarled rocks, a beachside cairn,
two fragments of one boulder fallen
into the sea, a common phenomenon,
though these mark old lovers who took care

of poor strangers, of whose devotion to the wayfarer
no more remains than two stones,
like relic holders enclosing bones,
that rise like the jagged back of a deep-sea creature.

2.
Unsatisfied by the villagers in the valley below
the cliffside cottage, hungry, disguised as beggars,
two gods knock on their door. The couple, slow
to answer because of their age, the fear that mars
all late in years, invite them in despite
the rags they wear. The odor of their filthy skin
and hair is old like theirs. There's something not right
about them, they can't say what, like the pin
prick sensation they feel when, in winter, a cold

wind seeps through chinks in their walls. They feed
them boiled cabbage and bacon chunks, a stew
already cooking on their stove, and a wine that indeed
is most poor but much better when filled anew
each time they finish a glass. A miracle. They know,
at last, who the beggars are and ask if it's so,

have they dined with gods? The two nod and give
them one wish. They reply, To die together, never
either to have to mourn for the other or to grieve.
Waves crash against the headlands. Light, water,
ocean are holy to them, sunset, the cry
of sea birds as they fly overhead. They're unafraid
of dying, they agree, as the gods disappear, like a sigh
heard late at night that maybe one lover has made
and then rolled over to sleep more soundly. As quickly,
they become two rocks, apart but together, islands
in a becalmed Pacific, craggy, rough-hewn, the sea
lit by luminous clouds, by a light that stands
outside the world, as gods do who've turned them into
stone, black as magma, gradually, over centuries,
to erode, to wash away, yet two altars, two

rocks, two lovers arising out of misty water, souls,
not shades or shadows. Ask the sand they will
become how it is like the sea or a shell like a wave,
how the dead recall the life they had, the bell tolls
of their days, and they will answer, We are the still-
ness within rivers, tides, winds, a sea-carved cave,
a storm, breezes on a sunny day, rustling leaves.
A wolf, a fox cub thankful for the meat it gnaws,
a bird soaring in air, a meteor, a cat's claws
teasing twine, a child on a swing, lovers lying side
by side, a father with his child on his back, a bride
awaiting her groom, a mother her baby, the crucified
one burning with desire, Ulysses re-sailing the ocean–
all will reply the same. Love moves without motion,
like stones in deep sea currents, altars to compassion.

A Boy's Secret Gardens

1.
Sick in bed, a wall, a trickling stream,
a door, a crippled boy, a boxwood maze,
stickseed burs clinging to my clothes,
laughter, grass, a labyrinth, the ways
out of it no one knows
except the crippled boy who will not tell
me because he wants me to stay,
to play
with him
in his secret garden.

2.
My puppet and I, its puppet master.
I work his strings,
making his legs walk, his arms swing,
his mouth move as freely
as mine, as a real boy's do.

            He touches me lovingly,
brushes my hair, embraces me, dashes faster
than I can to open the door,
magically there
way before me,

the puppet boy,
like a friend
I'd brought
to life I'd give my own life for
or somehow
send
him double the joy
he's given me, dancing in a corn field
like the scarecrow
in the scary *Wizard of Oz*.

3.
The stone well
in the center of it
is said to be bottomless.
There's no end to the loveliness
of April Collier's family's boxwood maze
in the rain,
the sweet, gentle spring rain that fell
on us before and falls again,
as familiar and surprising as the blaze
of sunlight breaking through clouds
afterwards
   while we find our way
out of it to the Collier patio where crisp cookies,
cinnamon buns, and lemonade
      always wait for us kids
who like to pretend we're imprisoned by some
mongrel monster in a maze
of boxwood and cypress trees
our own cunning frees us from.

4.
My dog Duke is run over by a truck
racing down Roslyn Road.
My father's working in his garden,
pruning camellias
or watering seedling rows he's hoed.

I hear Duke yelp when struck.
I can see a beam
of light like a truck's headlights
on in full daylight. Roses
splatter the window shield.

I touch the collar of my mother's fur
coat,
hoping it's true dogs go to heaven,
thinking about the brother

I never had, the empty field
behind the house we'd play in on hot
August afternoons before dinner beckoned us in.

5.
The fragrance, the heat of it,
a magnolia tree,
its perfume wafting everywhere,
strongest near the bench on which we sit
Kenny and I, one knee
touching the other,
two good buddies, brother
to brother,
friends who'll soon learn to hate.

A womanly scent's in the air,
a love I mean
to confess but can't, afraid it's true,
unable to bear
to tell it to him,
for him to hear it,
unable to wait.

He says we've sinned.
Rust-
tipped petals fall into our laps from a sudden gust
of wind.

6.
A boy of the plains in a straight back chair.
Life Magazine. He's looking where I can't see.
Pictures of him I hid in a closet where
no one would find them.
                              I'm free,
Saturdays, to work in my father's garden,
to please him,
azaleas, verben-
a, gardenias, roses.

Beautiful, with dark hair,
he stares into space, his eyes with the look
on my mother's face as she closes
her book
when it's stormy and unseasonably cold
outside and she's sad
for no reason and I'm told
nothing and so, thinking I've been bad,
try to wipe her tears away

while my father spends his day
attending to the rotten weather,
end of summer,
poisoning the snails devouring his garden.

7.
Incomplete, unfinishable,
which is what a garden is, what it must be,
some unreachable,
place, neither lost nor forgotten—

Tommy Gold in the changing room
his bold back side and tan line
turning away too soon
for me to see. It's a balmy
day in July,
an hour before noon,
the beach already crowded.

Nothing can redeem
the past.
It simply lasts
for the sake
of paradise. Like everything imaginary,
the lake
flows over the dam into the stream
below, its banks a garden
of ferns and wild grasses for teenage boys

like Tommy and me
to lie on,
in fantasy,
in desire unsatisfied
to infinity.

8.
If I let
my dreams go, will I sleep
as the old seem to sleep,
fitfully, for fear of not waking?

Or would it be bet-
ter to let them escape
into whatever they're forsaking
the present for, the fantasy
of living backward,
forward,
out of time,
the rhyme
of the end repeating the beginning,
a snake's tail in its mouth?

But suppose what I risk is the hazard
of death,
the garden
I'm searching for not at all
like heaven
but rank, thick with weeds
and underneath,
in the soil, no seeds
germinating,
the ivy I've climbed brown as the wall,
decayed as the dream I'm trying not to dream,
nightmare real and frightening?

Am I a child who's becoming someone he seems
not to be? Am I a boy with too many secrets?

9.
The trees are gradually greening,
their baby leaves
like a jade mist between earth
and a sky the blue
of faded porcelain.
The air shimmers with the sound
of faraway church bells, a temple's gong
that grieves
and rejoices for a morning too lovely to last.

A few
late budding flowers
rise like spirits above ground.
The dogwood, pink and white,
the hip-high boxwood
hedges, artfully trimmed,
smell as musty as rain
before rain falls, fragrant as teakwood.

It's a day good
for a walk in the park by the lake,
to revisit the plain,
lost truths of youth seen
in a photograph
or on an antique screen,
a stroll, a glimpse back home
to what ancient sages
would drink to and laugh about,

the past, old age,
late master
of gardens,
watching a flower
bloom as a stone does
on its own.

10.
 A youth that is
an old man's sleep, a dream
of honeysuckle, pine woods, a lake,
a cabin abandoned in the war,
lost images–soldiers' photographs, a jar
rank with rancid water, ripped pillow cases,
yellowed letters, their pencil marks
illegible, cracked plates, broken laces
dangling from muddy shoes.

                    A boy believes
in looming clouds, each afternoon a new
thunderstorm, the freedom of summertime,
in moccasins sliding through water, dew-
wet grass to lie on, red clay, lime-
stone caves to hide in, the air
gusting warm and strong,

the sun at twilight
shining through him as through mist,
the country
it sets in, the backwoods,
what he's never done
with,
          cooling breezes in September,
the secret they're promising
not to betray, the radiant after day
of fall's first storm's big blow,
the past that its winds restore,
the deserted garden
he's found in woods,
transcendently
in dreams to stay.

After the Beatitudes

1. Benediction

The world is a wonder of ordinariness. Every day
I'm surprised by its mere survival. Not miracles.
Just light and sky and sea. Blessed: *blessé.*
The earth is as scarred as we are, animals
that soon die. Waves are wounded, too, pounding
on beaches.

       Look at him, that man, your friend,
asleep in his bed, emaciated, sallow-eyed, his ring
so big on his finger it's fallen on the carpet. You'd lend
him your life if you could, you say. Would you?

              A soldier,
scared, sweating in his tent, cleaning his gun,
awaits his fate.

       Trapped, a woman's no other
choice. The high rise is brighter than the sun.
She must leap to her death or else burn alive.

After each death, what beneficence can survive?

By the lapping waves of the Galilee, barely waves
at all compared to the Pacific's, on a mountain,
in a plain, on the beach near my home, what saves
those oppressed by Rome, nations, rulers who gain
the world by enslaving it?

         Compassion, not power,
is blessing's kingdom. To bless is to change
body into soul, to make eternal any hour
of a day, to endow any moment with love.
              Arrange
some flowers in a vase, place them on a table

near a window. They blaze with new light
and color, perfuming the room. So grace is able,
like a Zen monk raking a garden, to set the heart right.

Gardener, water master, rabbi, make the spring rain turn
to stone, rocks flow. Bless the silence of pine and urn.

2. Blessed Are the Poor in Spirit

A priest leaves the priesthood because he no longer
believes. It's the demon, Monsignor says, he fled
to when he married a man.

                          Do people grow stronger
by what they need? How are the poor to be fed
when there's been a bad harvest?

                          Her child is napping
on her lap, far too skinny for a five year old.
What heart had she given him in her womb, wrapping
him in her body as if in a shroud? If she'd been told
his fate, would her loss be less great?

                          A desert kingdom
rises and falls like monarchs in medieval stories
of fortune's wheel. Its people's souls are numb
from constant war. In the west the search for glory's
a quest that leaves millions starved and needy.
Who will feed them? Where is the blessing of poverty?

Sort it out, if you can, mankind's impoverished spirit.
Confession of guilt is never enough, the Beckett
kit of a spindly tree and tramps that hit
you with their vaudeville punches on a stage set
built from despair, like a room where the Gestapo
tortured resistance fighters, one critic wrote.
Near the end of his life, a well-read man may know
only what he's jotted on cards, note after note.
116

Or know nothing at all, a spiritual ignorance
he can't fix before it is too late and his mind
a bad actor still. Dying, at his last performance,
he complains at the curtain, "I thought I'd find
salvation in disguises. All my life, I went
in costumes, a strutting player, lacking talent."

3. Blessed Are Those Who Mourn

A boy is stupefied as his special redwood, the tree
he's loved most out of a stand of a twenty or more,
collapses to the ground from old age, its badly
rotted roots no long able to support its weight. The floor
of the woods thunders at its fall.

                                    Childhood is a pagan
time when stones are inhabited by souls, a forest
by spirits. So it's been since the world began,
the cries of gods dying he hears in his dreams and can't rest
as they depart from their rocks and streams and lakes.

Mother in Aleppo, the dead boy in your arms
was a god, too, the son for whom your heart aches.

Or the daughter in the burning barn, the ruined farms
of Ukraine, the starving families.

                                    Gods live inside
all things or else we're deceived and childhood's lied.

There's a man on a tree who is bleeding everywhere.
A medic in two wars, a survivor of the retreat
from the Chosin Reservoir, a bit mad at the end, dar-
ing his enemies to come get him, his legs and feet
crippled by wounds left over from distant battles,
he dies in pain, his kidneys failing, the morphine
not working. His frail wife watches it, death rattles,
the final agony. *Stabat Mater.*

                    All death's a scene
from Golgotha. Cry for the dying neighbor in the back
of the ambulance, for the fat woman next door who choked
in her sleep, the everyday common losses that lack
for fame. We grieve for the earth, ourselves, tear-soaked
because we dwell in heartbreak.

                              Come, dove,
comforter. Help us mourn for all like those we love.

4. Blessed Are the Meek

The fragile woman on the fortieth floor adores
high rises They're the forest inside her that lets
her know peace, a seamstress whose chores
go unnoticed. As she stitches and sews, she forgets
herself. New York is her nature, each skyscraper
like the sequoias she's seen in pictures, heavenly
in their reaches, like the elevator that slowly lifts her
to the room she adorns with postcards of the city.

A sailor of the East China Sea suspects himself
of being no more than the water he sails on, the waves,
the wake, the foam, the storms, the looming shelf
he can see beneath the swirling currents, the caves
that roar with foreboding as his ship skirts the coast
where there's no working port, its harbors long lost.

A novice monk is copying out Latin poems
he's not able to comprehend. He makes no errors,
so great is his attention to his task. He roams
words, lines, pages like places on a map, doors
that open up new worlds. It's how he meditates,
each ink stroke an icon.

                    A man standing above
the Grand Canyon fears he might jump, but hesitates,
underserving of the grandeur he'd become.
118

                                        Does love
for the world mean to submit to it?

                           A child, a child
without parents, an abandoned child wants nothing
more than to be who she is, happy in the wild
place she lives in at night, asleep, a bird on the wing,
without belongings, just seeing all the air brings
with the wind, like a sparrow or wren, freely flying.

5. Blessed Are Those Who Hunger and Thirst for Righteousness

The Pacific is a good place to die by. It sings
to beaches of mutability, change, the illusory
dunes, the broken shells the high tide brings
in, brought home by beachcombers who see
in sand dollars' designs a pattern worth saving–
like an ancient sign that's outlasted the years
as pinnacles and boulders seem to, braving
new storms.

                           Time is whatever it is that fears
change, shifting sands, the lessons the sea
teaches, preaches to the young, to surfers sure
they're already immortal, don't need to be
tomorrow more than they are today, the cure
for whatever might kill them found in the bliss
of waves, the joy of nothing to thirst for or miss.

That which he should have done he did not do.
He longed to be good. But salvation came like a storm
at sea, the lure of the life to come in a view
so distant he couldn't see how it might harm
him where he lived, though he knew the sea
could be dangerous. Dry land is safer for love,
better still the high Sierras challenging mortality.

Why does a man hunger for anywhere free of
the earth? How is he to climb to the heavens,
to reach the sky's clarity on a cloudless day?

I remember, as a child, using the lens
of a magnifying glass and sun's rays on decay-
ing leaves to make them burn, the wind blow-
ing ashes into the sky where things set on fire go.

6. Blessed Are the Merciful

Whitman, Washington D.C.,1863

The war is over, but the hospitals are even fuller
than before. Most wounds are in the legs and arms,
but there is every kind of wound–none can deter
a minié ball or bullet–in every part–what harms
can be done to a man–of the body. Typhoid fever.
Diarrhoea. Catarrhal affections. Bronchitis. Pneumonia.
I stand tonight by the bedside–I'd crossed the river,
seen death in his face–of a new patient. I am a
brother, father, mother, lover who holds his hand.
I soothe his pain. I always kiss him. He does me.
In an adjourning ward, his brother suffers. I stand
over him and touch him. One is a Unionist, Army
of the Potomac. The other Secesh. In the same battle,
both were hit. Each dies inside me, Yankee, Rebel.

A Young Nurse, San Francisco, 1983

I'm just a young nurse, a novice frightened of
Ward 5B, the men, boys, in it not much older
than I am. A few are younger. Some doctors shove
me aside when I'm in their way. I drink water
from the fountain, read a chart, fix my cap,
then knock before I go in. Sometimes he's shit

himself or coughed up blood. The room stinks. On his lap,
lies a tray of uneaten food. His sunken eyes are lit
by fear, like a skunk or raccoon's bright in the dark
behind my apartment. For the first time, I risk it.
I touch his forehead, try to soothe him, remark
how his fever's gone down, comment how the cit-
y is beautiful, how fine the weather is. The sky's
so blue today. He cries. Or it's me who cries.

7. Blessed Are the Pure in Heart

Never be too pure, Lawrence railed, it pollutes
the blood.

          Or kills, like the purity that murders
Jews, Slavs, Gypsies, Gays, that shoots
the lame and infirm, the blind, the deaf, furthers
science by dissecting them alive in labs.

                                        Purity
is the law of tyrants, the demand, the rule that all
be identical, the same plains, mountains, sea
they must come from, the same history, the same call
of the past their one true home, their harmony.

Never be too pure. It is a species of pride,
like a chastity of spirit that means to see
no one is happy, none free to think, that must hide
inside robes, burqas, habits, clerical collars.

Purity is the claim of men who start wars.
Drink. The water here, this high in the mountains,
this far from roads, is free from pollution.
The air smells of pine, rhododendron, recent rains,
the sweet decay of last year's leaves. The sun
is steady in the sky, as if ordered again by
Joshua not to move. The birds are still

as stones. No bushes rustle.

                              Be quiet. Try
to find in this silence your own stillness, the will-
lessness of creation, of his yielding to the cross
not to sacrifice himself but because he must,
a choice not his but for which he's been chosen, a loss
of life all must submit to, to become dust
again, the pure impurity of death,

                              Socrates
owing a cock to Asclepius, leaving Crito to pay his fees.

8. Blessed Are the Peacemakers

The world is war-weary. Children of God, men
die in your absence. The worst have too much heart
for battle and killing. It's now as it's always been.
Innocents flee for their lives by camel, ox-cart,
raft, or on foot, emptying cities for mountain tops,
rocky islands, unmapped forests, improvised refugee
camps across the border. Nothing, no one stops
the slaughter. Just a few find their way to safety.

Suppose the soul could nourish gardens, be
fertile soil for roses, jonquils, dahlias, lilies.
Suppose it could wander there freely, in beauty.

But an angel with flames stands at the gate. He's
expelled all, a lord with a sword in his hand.
The peace of paradise is too holy to understand.
There's been another drowning at Ocean Beach. The sea
is not peaceful. Nature's, too, is a war-weary world.

You remember how it was, after the victory,
in the first weeks, the parades, the bands, the unfurled
flags and banners? Or so it was shown on the news.

In fact, it was a quieter thing, your return
as if from the grave, an m.i.a. You didn't choose
to disappear, of course, nor want us to learn
you were still alive by knocking on our door.
Yet there you were, like a ghost of yourself, borne back
to us like a body swept in by waves. It's a poor
way to think of peace. I mean only as a lack
of fighting, of casualty lists, as a loved one you pray
so hard to believe is alive you see him every day.

9. Blessed Are Those Who Are Persecuted for Righteousness' Sake

No more lore of good wounds, of martyrs broken
on wheels, shot through with arrows, burned over
coals or on stakes coated with pitch, no more men
wearing jackets loaded with bombs for the favor
of their lord. No more cults of saints, stoic in
their fervor, tortured, suffering without showing
any fear, appearing happy, dying with a grin
on their faces as the fire below them is growing
more fierce. No more excuses for further persecutions
by celebrating torment, pain as proof of faith.

Just thirteen, a boy lies sleepless in bed. Confusions,
dread, assail him. Belief has failed him. Death
invades his prayers. No longer blessed, shriven,
confessed by a priest, how can he be forgiven?

A sad-eyed old man, he waits in his book-laden room
for death. He knows it might hesitate for quite
a while. Yet, like a grim statistic, it is loom-
ing over him, each new calculation always right
no matter how he runs the numbers. Reason
is both closest friend and persecutor. He's a scholar
without renown who throughout his life has been
faithful to the enlightenment, a sort of martyr,
as he sees it, to its rigorous logic. The world's sin-

less, but guilty of crimes, the worst of them war
and genocide. He knows too much to believe in
God, can see clearly what lies ahead of and far
behind him. All life's hopeless. And yet addressed
by nothing, no lord, why does he feel it's blessed?

10. Dietrich Bonhoeffer

For blessed are the poor in spirit, those who mourn,
the meek, those who hunger after righteousness,
the merciful, the pure in heart, the peacemakers, those torn
from righteous lives who are persecuted.

                                        He bless-
es them as he climbs the gallows' stairs, long
imprisoned, pastor, plotter against one of history's
vilest tyrants. Protestor, who knew it wrong
to murder, of course, yet he took that sin, glory's
ruin upon himself. If not a saint, a martyr,
a holy man, who was he?

                        Religionless religion,
the enigmatic words he used to stir
up debate. Might it mean freedom, reason
enough to question all creeds, to think everything
from mountain or plain back to faith's beginning?

What did he observe, what new, as the noose was placed
round his neck? What music, hymn, spiritual, if any,
played in his head? No one can guess what he faced
the moment before he was killed, what he could see.
To be faithful all you needed were the beatitudes,
he'd said. In the end, was he blessed? Perhaps they
lingered on his lips, the bible's words, the feuds
fighting inside him pacified. No one can say
what a man's, a woman's death is. Religionless religion.

The son, in Mark's dark vision of him on the cross,
abandoned, forsaken, cries out like a man in prison
who's guilty of no crime, yet condemned to the loss
of his life.

      Is it your hoplessness you're confessing to?
Is it your despair, your dying cry, that blesses you?

Humiliation as an Earnest of the Lord

1.
The fog-drenched cliff's ledges are slippery to climb
from the beach or to walk down, ninety feet or more
if you lose your footing, board in hand. Yet longtime
surfers prefer to paddle out there far from shore.

The crescent's clouded in, windy, as they put on,
strip off their wet suits.
                I feel like a child again,
counting the cliff's steps like rungs on a ladder, the sun
blinding me as I fell from the barn I'd been forbidden
to climb, the shock of no light all I saw as I hit
the ground and went black inside. Immensity
had claimed me.

            Wave after wave, a rhythm to submit
to riding the tube. Inside it, what do surfers be-
come? Is it like the thrill of wind in a sail, the sea's
power overwhelming your freedom, not your pride's
but its will you're joyfully riding, what pleases
it enthralling you,
               the ocean's heroic tides?

2.
More war stories on the news this morning.

                  It's high tide.
I follow gulls' tracks in the sand. The sea as it storms
is eyeing me. The hour is solemn.

           If I died
here, would I be changed into water, a wave that forms
me? Or become a sand dollar, or, floating alone,
a jar tossed that breaks on the beach, driftwood,
a shell, dried seaweed, a water-worn stone,
some discardable thing, neither sinister nor good?

In a cove by the Cliff House, a giant craggy boulder
watches me, suspicious I might soon be carved
from it, not into a portrait, head and shoulder,
but ground to a skinny slab, famished pebbles, a starved
slag heap.

The day's dark gray. It's changing back to
summer.

I'm a mad pack of dogs barking at waves,
the pelicans that escape them, the venomous blue
anemones that flower in tide pools by cliffside caves.

3.
A moon white chill's in the air. The starless city
sky's lit from below by streetlights, by San Francisco's
nightly glow, its dread of dark, its petty
infidelities, the stories it repeats down rows
upon rows of houses,
                              like those I've told of my-
self, living my days as if I believed them,
the fictional past, the lies a person goes by
because all he maintains he's been, as at a whim
of fate, is being taken away or is certain
to fall, to fail in the draw of a card, a match
of a game he'll have to quit playing since it's plain
by the odds that he'll lose.

There must be a catch,
some way out, a better future I wouldn't refuse,
not like this one, reflected in the lights of a city
burning for the show of it.

But why must I choose
between a world on fire and a darkening sea?

4.

You walked me to my home, kissed me, then left.
Now you are the one I tell them the stories about,
the beauty I once knew, sky blue eyes, cleft
chin, a moving man's muscles and grip.

                                   What doubt
I have is not mine only. I am eyed by a death
that likes lying about me, is my daily enemy,
who is taking my fantasies, my pride, my breath
away
          as you still do, my love, my unreality.

What remains? My life is failing me, a tide
on its way out, cleaning the beach, wiping
it free from detritus for another day, the wide
strand white as snow
                        as if there were nothing
it's left behind but glittering sand, the colorless,
clear white sky, the piercing sun.
                               Humiliation
is like a gift sometimes, a new nakedness,
the soul prepared, stripped bare for its uncreation.

Acknowledgements:

A few of these poems have appeared in literary magazines or books:

"After a Schwarzwald Legend," "Darl Bundren in France," "Deconsecration," and "Eight Voices after the War" in *Danse Macabre*, "Stone Altars" and "Three Prayers" in *The Light Ekphrastic*, "Four Showers" in *The Outrider Review*, "My Mother in Her Dotage and the Kindness of the Lord" in *The Raintown Review*, and "An Old Man Sleeps in Yadkin County" in *Visions International*. "Galen's Glasses" was first published in *Maenam, Of Water Of Light, Photographs by Galen Garwood*. "Thirteen Fragments from a Lost Gospel" is an extensive revision of *From a Lost Gospel of Mark*, published as a chapbook by 2RiverView.

Thanks to Nathan Wirth for his stunning, moving photographs, the inception and inspiration for many of these poems.

Thanks as well to Helen Alford, Steve Arkin, Gerald Coble, Kevin Dyer, Galen Garwood, David Morris, Robert Mohr, Jon O'Bergh, Corb Rouse, Elizabeth Spinner, Bradley Strahan, and Lindley Young for their reading my work while it was in progress, watching over and guiding me through many revisions.

Thanks to Clarinda Harriss of BrickHouse, poet, editor, now friend, and a recurrent wonder. This book could not exist without her generosity of spirit.

And to Atticus Carr, my husband, thanks for the nearly three decades of life together and for the constancy of his kindness and love.

Peter Weltner has published five books of fiction, including *The Risk of His Music* and *How the Body Prays,* three poetry chapbooks, three collaborations with the artist Galen Garwood, most recently *Water's Eye*, and three full length collections of poems, *News from the World at My Birth: A History*, *The Outerlands*, and *To the Final Cinder*, the latter two also from BrickHouse Books. A graduate of Hamilton College and Indiana University, he taught for thirty seven years at San Francisco State University. He and Atticus Carr live in San Francisco, steps away from the ocean.